DID NOT ENTER

Misadventures in Running, Cycling and Swimming
(Book Five in the DNF Series)

George Mahood

Copyright © 2021 by George Mahood

All rights reserved. This book or any portion thereof may not be reproduced or used in any manner whatsoever without the express written permission of the author except for the use of brief quotations in a book review.

This edition published 2021 by George Mahood.

www.facebook.com/georgemahood
www.instagram.com/georgemahood
www.twitter.com/georgemahood
www.georgemahood.com

ONE

'I've got a plan. Do you want to come on a cycle trip with me to France?' I said, excitedly proposing my idea to my wife, Rachel.

'France? When?'

'Next week.'

During the four previous summer holidays, we had travelled to France with our three children for a couple of weeks' camping. Each time we disembarked the ferry in our car, I noticed a handful of cyclists standing with their bikes on the car deck, about to begin what looked like a cycling holiday. We had been taking our bikes with us to France, but there was something alluring about only having a bike. I was envious of their freedom, and the simplicity of travelling with just a couple of panniers or a small backpack. It brought back memories of my Land's End to John O'Groats adventure when, for a few weeks, life felt strangely simple. Each day was about cycling, eating and sleeping and there was little else to worry about. On our most recent holiday to France, I looked back in the rear-view mirror at our overflowing van, filled to the brim with clothes, food and camping equipment, and although I truly loved our family holidays, I also craved the idea of seeing France from the (dis)comfort of a bike saddle.

Rachel and I had just heard the news that Doug – our neighbour from Northampton – had died. Doug had enjoyed reading my books and hearing all about the adventures we had been on. He had taken up cycling again in his 70s to try to keep fit and often talked about heading off on his own bike adventure. I decided I should take my bike on a spontaneous cycle trip to France; partly in Doug's memory, but also because his death had once again reminded me how important it is that we should make the most of our health.

There are two ferry routes out of Plymouth in Devon. One goes to Roscoff in the north-west corner of France, the other to Santander in Spain. One day I would like to cycle from one to the other. But for now, Roscoff seemed ambitious enough. While checking the ferry website, I noticed one lone ferry scheduled from Plymouth to Saint-Malo: the beautiful walled town on the northern coast of France. I knew it was possible to get a ferry from Portsmouth to Saint-Malo, but I had never heard of a crossing from Plymouth before. There were a couple of things about the scheduled ferry that confused me. First, it was in early November, which must be one of the least popular times of year for people to holiday in France. And second, there was not a single scheduled crossing coming back the other way from Saint-Malo to Roscoff. So, you either had to go to Saint-Malo and stay there forever, or come home via a different port.

I tried to curtail my enthusiasm about the crossing in case it turned out to be a glitch on the website. But I phoned Brittany Ferries and they confirmed it was available to book and explained that it was not a normal scheduled crossing, but they had to shuffle their boats around between ports ready for the winter timetable.

My excitement levels rose further when I read about the Eurovelo 4. The Eurovelo 4 (EV4) is a signposted long-distance cycle route that extends 4,000k from Roscoff in France, to Kiev in the Ukraine. Crucially, it also passes through Saint-Malo. So, in theory, I (or we, if I could persuade someone to join me) could get a ferry to Saint-Malo and then spend a few days cycling a section of the EV4 to the port in Roscoff to catch a ferry home. The lone ferry to Saint-Malo departed Plymouth on the night of Thursday, November 1st, but because of the reduced winter timetable, the only suitable return journey departed Roscoff at 3pm on Sunday, November 4th. This section of the EV4 hugs the north coast of France for about 250 miles, and I (or we) would have just 2.5 days to complete the distance. The direct road route – avoiding the wiggly coastline – was significantly shorter, so there should always be a contingency plan if the longer route proved too ambitious.

I hoped Rachel would feel as excited about the idea as I did.

'Er... not really,' she said, without a hint of enthusiasm.

'Oh. I thought you enjoyed cycling in France?'

'I do like cycling in France. In August. Not November.'

I explained the specifics of the trip I had planned, hoping it would change her mind. It didn't work.

'I enjoy going for short little rides to get croissants or ice creams,' she said. 'Not 250 miles in two-and-a-half days. You should go, though.'

'I don't want to go on my own. I want to go with you. And I've never been abroad on my own before.'

'What about the three months you spent in America on your own?'

'Oh yeah, I forgot about that. Well, apart from that.'

'Why don't you see if any of your friends want to go with you?'

'Yeah, I could do. But it's next week! And they would have to take the Friday off work.'

I sent out a message to a few friends, apologising for the brief notice, but seeing if anyone was interested in getting a November ferry to France with me and cycling 250 miles in 2.5 days. Understandably, the replies came back about work and family commitments. But then Simon – my Cotswold 133 and Exeter Marathon friend – replied saying that it sounded awesome, but he had to try and rearrange a few work and childcare commitments first. I thought this was perhaps him just being polite and delaying his excuses, but a few hours later he replied again. He was in. Simon and I were going to France.

Did Not Enter

A week later, we parked up the van in Plymouth, unloaded our bikes (paying for parking for three days was more expensive than the ferry crossing), and made our way to the terminal. Simon and I were both riding road bikes, and, with no pannier racks, were carrying a small backpack each, containing a single change of clothes and an assortment of token bike repair bits. In the terminal, we followed the sign for foot passengers, wheeled our bikes up a flight of stairs, and then to an information desk.

'Are we in the right place? Do cyclists count as foot passengers?' I asked, already knowing the answer by the look of surprise on the lady's face.

'No, sorry. You need to go through check-in with the cars.'

We wheeled our bikes back down the stairs and around to the other side of the building to queue up at passport control with the cars. Except there were no other cars. We presented our passports to the man and double-checked the ferry was running as planned.

'Why is it so quiet?' asked Simon.

'It's not a very popular route,' said the man. 'There won't be many on the boat tonight.'

This was an understatement. The boat was fully staffed, yet there seemed to be fewer than 50 passengers on a ship with a capacity of 2,400. There were genuinely more crew than passengers.

I feel a tremendous sense of excitement stepping onto a ferry that I don't get when boarding an aeroplane. I am not a particularly nervous flier, but there is always a slight level of unease when I remember I am sitting in a metal tube tens of thousands of feet in the air. I don't get any of that sense of anxiety on a ferry. As soon as I set foot on a boat, I am on holiday.

We boarded at 7.30pm and had over an hour before departure. There were two bars and a restaurant open, so we did a mini pub crawl starting with a beer in the restaurant, moving on to the lounge bar and ending with three more pints in the main bar which was hosting a quiz night to about a dozen passengers. After five pints, Simon and I were both well and truly into the holiday spirit, forgetting the slight matter of a lot of cycling miles over the following few days.

At about 10.30pm, we gathered our things and went to find our cabin.

'Oh, I didn't realise we were sharing a bed,' said Simon, opening the door to reveal one tiny single bunk.

'Neither did I,' I laughed. 'I definitely booked a two-berth. At least, I think I did.'

'Well, it looks like there's just the one bed. Oh well.'

The cabin bed was so small that it would have been impossible to fit us both in, and there was not enough floor space for either of us to lie down. Although, given my state of inebriation, I would have happily slept slumped against the wall. As the ferry was so empty, I was confident they would have a spare cabin, so decided to go and ask.

Just as I turned to leave, Simon said, 'Hang on, what's

this?'

He turned a small handle on one of the roof panels and a hidden bed dropped magically from the ceiling.

'Woooow, that's genius,' I said. 'I don't think there's any way I could climb up there, though. Bagsie having the bottom bunk.'

In our drunken revelry, Simon and I compared the kit we had brought with us. He proudly showed off his small folding travel toothbrush, which he had bought specifically to save space (because toothbrushes notoriously take up such a vast amount of room). I had a normal sized toothbrush, but my frazzled brain was envious of Simon's. So, I snapped the head clean off my toothbrush. Simon burst out laughing at the pathetic handle-less brush head I was left holding.

'Now YOURS is the stupidly big toothbrush,' I slurred.

Brushing my teeth for the next few days using just a toothbrush head proved really annoying. I wouldn't recommend it as a space-saving tactic.

Five pints the night before a big bike ride is not ideal preparation, but it was all part of the experience. Thankfully, it was a very calm crossing and we both slept solidly but woke with sore heads to the piped harp music of the Brittany Ferries alarm clock. We had a full English breakfast followed by croissants and pain au chocolate, reinforcing our Anglo-Franco bonds, and headed down to the car deck to be reunited with our bikes. We wheeled them to the front of the short queue of cars, and when they lowered the ramp down to the dock at 8.00am, we were the first off the ferry, through passport control, and into the crisp November morning.

The beautiful city of Saint-Malo has a rich history and has been an important settlement since the 1st century BC. As we cycled through the streets, it felt like it was all just as it would have been hundreds of years ago. The city was largely destroyed, however, by American bombing and British naval gunfire while under German occupation in the Second World War. It was rebuilt over the following decades and is now one of the most popular sights in France. We had a long day ahead and there was unfortunately no time to linger.

The Eurovelo 4 promised to be marked the entire way with EV4 signs, but my limited research had suggested it was often a twisty and convoluted route. I had made a few contingency plans just in case. As well as a basic paper map, I also downloaded a digital file of the route onto my phone, so that, if lost, we could see where we were in relation to the route. I had also recently bought a new GPS watch, and it had a 'navigation' function. Using some tech wizardry, I also transferred the digital route to my watch, and had optimistically assumed this would display some sort of map of the route on my watch. I tested it out for the very first time after disembarking the ferry in Saint-Malo and was disappointed to discover it was actually just a single red line on an otherwise black watch face.

'Stupid piece of shit,' I said. 'I paid a fortune for this watch, and all I get is a crappy red line. How are we supposed to navigate with this?'

My initial disappointment quickly lifted when I realised how effective this simple red line was. The line was the route we were supposed to follow. If we detoured off this line – by missing a turning or taking the wrong exit on a roundabout – the watch vibrated, and a red dot appeared on the watch face to show me where we were in relation to the route. It was very simple, but extremely effective. 250 miles in 2.5 days was going to be very ambitious, so it was reassuring to know we wouldn't have to do too much in the way of navigating, and we would hopefully soon know about it if we strayed off track.

We could not have hoped for better weather. It was the beginning of November, so a little chilly, but there was not a cloud in the sky, nor a breath of wind, and it was forecast to stay that way for the next 48 hours. We would spend two nights in France but had yet to book any accommodation as we didn't know how far we would be able to cycle each day. We planned to get as far as we could and see where we ended up. It might prove to be a bit of a logistical challenge finding somewhere to stay, as the route passed through mostly rural areas, with few villages and even fewer sizable towns.

Finding our first EV4 sign within a couple of minutes

of leaving Saint-Malo's ferry port was a momentous moment.

'Get in! The route does exist,' I said. 'I wondered if maybe it was all imaginary.'

'I'm glad you're telling me this now,' said Simon.

We skirted along the banks of the La Rance estuary, through the beautiful villages of Saint-Jouan-des-Guérets, Les Gastines and Saint-Suliac. Saint-Suliac was especially striking, with the outside walls of several houses draped with old fishing nets as decoration. These villages are popular destinations in the summer for people taking excursions from Saint-Malo. But on a cold Friday morning in November, we had them to ourselves.

We crossed the river at the Pont Saint-Hubert before turning off the road onto a gravel track and around the edge of a village. We quickly learned that the Eurovelo 4 was designed to do everything possible to avoid going on any roads other than extremely minor ones. On one hand, this was wonderful as we were always in the beautiful French countryside with no traffic to contend with and rarely any other people. But it also meant it was very slow going. These off-road sections were rarely surfaced and often gravelly, muddy or rocky. It would have been far better suited to a mountain bike, rather than the road bikes we had naively brought. There were a few occasions when we arrived at a main road junction (when I say main road, I mean a road with lines in the middle. There were very few cars on ANY of the roads in France. Even the main ones), but rather than use a section of this main road, the EV4 would turn off just before and follow bumpy and hilly farm tracks in a big, convoluted loop, only to pop out about 100 metres down the same road.

'Hang on,' said Simon, pointing up the road. 'Isn't that the junction we were at about 45 minutes ago?'

'Er, yeah. It is. I didn't realise we did all of that last section just to avoid this stretch of nice, quiet, perfectly smooth road.'

Simon rolled his eyes. 'I know, I know, we've got to stick to the route.'

I don't enjoy being a stickler for the rules. Ok, I do. But we had come to France to cycle from Saint-Malo to Roscoff following the EV4. If we started taking shortcuts so early in the trip, then it would be too tempting to take them at every opportunity. We could just jump on one of the main highways and be in Roscoff in half the time. But where would be the fun in that? Despite the tough off-road sections, it was such a joy to be cycling in France and we were both loving every minute.

Packing for three days' cycling with a small backpack had been a challenge. The weather forecast looked promising for the first two days with some rain predicted for Sunday. It was still early November, and likely to be cold, so I opted to wear a pair of long cycling trousers I had owned for a few years but never worn. Within the first hour, I regretted my decision. The squidgy padded bottom kept squidging up my bottom and my legs felt unnecessarily hot. I wear shorts throughout the year – and always during exercise – so was not used to cycling with my legs covered. After a quick roadside wee (I decided against doing it down my leg this time like in the Cotswold 113), I changed out of my cycling trousers and put on a pair of minimally padded cycling shorts instead and felt a lot better.

We spent the morning cycling through beautiful old villages – most consisting of only a few houses – and through farmland still bursting with produce waiting to be harvested. We crossed the river Frémur and continued for many miles with fields stretching either side of us. The navigation was easy. Every junction had a small EV4 logo and an arrow letting us know we were going the right way. And on the few occasions we missed a turn or had somehow strayed off course, my watch gave a little warning, and we could correct our mistake.

We stopped for a quick rest on a bridge over the Arguenon estuary with fishing and sailing boats moored below us, and the ruins of Chateau du Guildo on the banks of the river. We had brought a couple of cereal bars to tide us over but would buy food and refill our water bottles along the way.

Soon after midday Simon and I tried and failed to find something to eat at a couple of boulangeries on the outskirts of Notre-Dame-du-Guildo – both closed for lunch – so continued west along the EV4, now severely flagging and eager to find food. I had stashed away some emergency salt and vinegar Hula Hoops if things got desperate, but I wasn't ready to bring them out just yet.

Fortunately, a little patisserie called La Madeleine in the pretty town of Matignon was doing a roaring trade by making the bold step of being open at lunchtime. Simon and I ordered a filled baguette each, crisps, a pain au chocolate, a can of Coke and asked them to fill our bottles with tap water. We sat on benches outside next to a quaint little fountain to eat our well-earned lunch.

'Oh god that's good,' said Simon. 'Why is it that a sandwich du jambon tastes SO much better than a ham sandwich?'

'I don't know, but it definitely does. Even de l'eau tastes better than water.'

We sat in silence for a while, both hugely content with our situation.

'This pain au chocolate is damn good too,' I said. 'Almost as good as the ones I had in a holiday park in Croyde.'

'Croyde? As in North Devon Croyde?'

'Yep, that's the one.'

'Is the holiday park famous for its pain au chocolate?'

'No, but it should be.'

The morning's scenery had been delightful, but it was all just a prelude for the afternoon. We cycled through the town of Pléboulle (which, incidentally, sounds like something the French would shout at the start of a pétanque match), and onto the coast road at Port à la Duc. The two kilometre stretch between Port à la Duc and Le Port Nieux is one of the most pleasant I had ever cycled along. The road tightly hugs the coastline, with only a small wall separating the land from the sea and the foreshore below. We saw just one car along this entire stretch.

'This sure beats my usual Friday afternoons at work,' said Simon. 'I'd be sitting in some boring strategy meeting in the office at the moment. What would you be doing?'

'Just a normal day, probably. Sitting at home wallowing in self-loathing for not writing as many words as I planned.'

'Jeez, you're making my meeting sound strangely appealing.'

The EV4 cuts across the headland from Port Nieux, missing out the spectacular castle of Fort la Latte – which I was lucky enough to visit with the family on another holiday. We rejoined the coast at Cap Fréhel and I immediately added this road to my list of personal favourites too.

The road sits high on the pink sandstone cliffs, with the wild English Channel crashing onto the rocks below. The French call the arm of the Atlantic Ocean that separates France and England la Manche, meaning '*the sleeve*'. I much prefer this to the English Channel and am going to start using it from now on.

The Cap Fréhel lighthouse stood proudly at the end of the headland to our right, but we turned left, the road dipping and climbing past several white sandy beaches.

There were many other people out walking at Cap Fréhel and the occasional cyclist, and Simon and I both felt extremely privileged to be spending our day with such a spectacular backdrop.

This stretch of coastline is reminiscent of some of South Devon and Cornwall's rugged terrain. Geologists have recently suggested that hundreds of millions of years ago, the south west of England was part of the landmass that now includes France. It crashed into what is now Britain, and as it retreated over millions of years, it left Devon and Cornwall stuck to Britain.

In the late afternoon we reached the seaside town of Sables D'or les Pins, which I had visited in the summer with Rachel and the kids. We stayed for four nights at a campsite in Erquy about four miles west of here, and we cycled to Sables D'or Les Pins one day for an ice cream. I had been talking to Simon about this ice cream when we passed our first signpost to Sables D'or Les Pins, and the promise of one had boosted our declining morale. It turned out all ice cream sellers were closed. Which was unsurprising, as it was November. We followed the EV4 out over the sand flats and up through the pine forests to the town of Erquy, where thankfully we found ice cream.

Simon had been in fine spirits all day considering we had covered over 50 miles of very tough terrain. To stand any chance of following the EV4 all the way to Roscoff by Sunday, we needed to cover many more miles before the end of the day. I hoped to at least get to Saint-Brieuc, which was still another 25 miles away.

We leaned our bikes against the sea wall by the sandy beach of Plage de Caroual. We finished our ice creams, had a quick swig of water, ate a weird French pastry thing, and then I assumed we would head on our way. Simon had other ideas. He had taken off his rucksack and helmet and was lying down on the sea wall.

'Are you ready to make a move, buddy?' I said.

'Yeah, can you just give me a minute? I just need a quick nap.'

'Sure,' I laughed, assuming by 'nap' he meant rest. But seconds later his breathing noticeably changed, and he had fallen into a deep sleep. I took the opportunity to use a nearby toilet and then had a little wander on the beach, before nervously looking at my watch. It was 4.30pm. We only had about an hour and a half of daylight left, and a lot more cycling still to do.

I returned to the car park 15 minutes after leaving and found Simon still in a deep sleep. *How long is a quick nap?* I gave my feet a subtle scuff in the gravel which stirred Simon from his slumber.

'Right. I'm good to go,' he said, jumping to his feet and fastening his helmet.

'Are you sure?'

'Absolutely. It's not far to go, is it?'

'Um... no... not far at all,' I lied.

From Plage de Caroual, we followed dirt tracks and back roads to the stylish-looking town of Pléneuf-val-andré. The sun was low in the sky ahead of us, soaking everything in a deep orange glow and casting long beautiful shadows on the ground behind us. It made for extremely enjoyable cycling, but it was also a stark reminder that the sun would soon dip below the horizon.

I was hopeful we would eventually make it to Saint-Brieuc, so we pulled over and I booked us a cheap hotel room using my phone, just to give us the peace of mind that we would have a bed waiting for us when we arrived. Our hopes lifted each time we saw a road sign telling us it was only 5 kilometres to Saint-Brieuc, only for the EV4 to turn off the road and wind its way into the middle of Je-Ne-Sais-Pas Ville.

'My legs are almost done,' said Simon.

'Mine too. We're nearly there,' I said.

'You've been saying that for a while now, mate.'

'I know, but I mean it this time. I think those lights ahead are Saint-Brieuc.'

'Excellent. And is our hotel in the centre of town?'

'No, it's on the outskirts of the city so hopefully even closer than the centre.'

The sun had set a while ago, and with five miles still to go, we were cycling in complete darkness. We both had lights and were wearing high-vis jackets, but the route we were following was very uneven, and would have been extremely challenging to cycle on even in the daytime. We pushed our bikes up a short hill to meet the oasis of a well-lit road on the edge of Saint-Brieuc. From here, the EV4 was going to skirt around the southern edge of the city. Our hotel was not on the EV4, so we needed to deviate from the route. I found our hotel on Google Maps and then selected the cycle option.

'1.6 miles! Woo hoo!' I shouted as we pedalled off down the nice smooth road. 'SAINT-BRIEUC, BABY!'

From here, we hoped to follow perfectly surfaced tarmac roads all the way to the hotel. Google Maps had other ideas.

'SAINT-BRIEUC, BABY!' shouted Simon behind me.

Just then, I heard the Google Maps lady say something to me, and I swear there was a slightly mocking tone to her voice.

'Oh bollocks,' I said, coming to a stop. 'Apparently we missed a turning back there.'

'I didn't see a turning,' said Simon.

'Well, that's what my phone says.'

We cycled back up the way we came, and about 50m along the road there was a narrow gravel track leading up the hill to our right that had been invisible in the darkness.

'Up there? Really?' said Simon. 'I thought you said the hotel was only a couple of miles away.'

'It is. 1.5 miles now, according to the Google Maps lady.'

'And this gravel track is going to lead us there quicker than the road?'

'I guess so. It's the way she wants us to go.'

'But surely there must be a way to get there on roads?'

'Maybe, but I've never cycled in Saint-Brieuc before. What happens if we follow the road and then it suddenly turns into a motorway or something?'

Simon hung his head in resignation.

It turned out that the hotel I had booked was indeed on the outskirts of Saint-Brieuc, but it was also at the top of a massive hill. This had not been obvious from looking at the notoriously flat Google Maps. To either side of us, the suburbs of Saint-Brieuc were bright and bustling, but we were on a rural dirt track that had somehow survived all of the surrounding urbanisation.

'Just a mile to go,' I called back to Simon.

He just gave a sort of grunt.

It was time for a lift.

It was time for the Hula Hoops.

I tore open the packet and as Simon came to a stop next to me, I could see the excitement on his face even in the darkness.

'Oh. My. God,' he said. 'Thank you.'

We devoured the pack in seconds.

It was definitely the toughest mile since leaving Saint-Malo, and not how we expected our day's ride would end. We eventually reached tarmac again and skirted past a series of different hotels before turning into the car park of ours. We had covered 75 miles – most of which were off-road – following a lot of beer the night before. We had both done very well.

'We did it!' I said to Simon, giving him a big hug.

'Thank god for that. Sorry I got a bit grumpy towards the end there. That was really tough.'

'You've got nothing to apologise for. It was a really tough day. Sorry if I was annoying about insisting that we stick to the route.'

'Well, you were a bit, but you were right. That's what we came here for. It has been an awesome day.'

'Look, there's a pizzeria next door. Let's check in and then go eat.'

The hotel had nowhere for us to store our bikes, so we carried them up the four flights of stairs and locked them to the railings of the motel-style exterior corridor outside our room.

After a quick shower and a change into our 'evening wear', we were ready to hit the pizzeria. My 'evening wear' consisted of a long-sleeved t-shirt, a clean pair of shorts and a pair of flip-flops. We had given our cycling shorts and t-shirts a rinse in the shower and then hung them on the radiator to dry.

The pizzeria next door was surprisingly busy, but they gave us a table and we ordered two large cokes and a bottle of red wine. I went for a la Reine pizza, topped with ham, mushrooms and olives.

'What is Lan Dooley de Gwee Meeney?' said Simon.

'Where's that?'

'Fourth pizza down.'

'L'andouille de Guémené. I've heard of that. I think it's

a speciality Brittany sausage. It's supposed to be really nice.'

'Cool, I'll go for a Lan Dooley de Gwee Meeney pizza then.'

The wine arrived. I'm not sure if we had chosen a particularly good bottle, or if it was just because of our tough day's cycling, or that we were effectively on holiday in France, but it was the most delicious wine I had ever tasted. I sat there savouring every sip when a really revolting smell filtered into my nostrils. I looked around at the nearby tables and nobody seemed to be eating anything other than normal looking pizzas. The smell became even more prominent, and I noticed Simon's face twitching slightly as he too caught a whiff.

'What is that?' he said.

'I don't know. It smells like fart and death.'

Moments later, a waitress placed a magnificent-looking pizza on my plate. Thin and crispy, generous with the toppings and spilling over the edge of the plate.

'Merci madam,' I said.

'Cor, that looks bloody good,' said Simon. 'Definitely worth cycling 75 miles for.'

And then another server arrived and presented Simon with his pizza. From the moment she placed it on the table, it was clear that this was the source of the smell. Simon's pizza looked like a normal pizza in many ways. It was cooked perfectly, generously sized, and steaming hot. But piled on top of it were about six big mounds of what looked like doner kebab meat. Now I'm fond of doner kebabs and have even had a few doner kebab pizzas in my time. But I have never had a doner kebab that smelled like this. This wasn't doner kebab. This was L'andouille de Guémené, whatever the fuck that was.

'Oh my god. Was the smell of fart and death coming from your pizza?' I said.

'It appears so,' said Simon, trying to play it cool.

I looked around, and a few of the nearby diners were looking our way and wincing slightly. This was too much even for their more sophisticated French palates.

'You said you've had it before and it's really nice, yeah?' said Simon, remaining optimistic, cutting up his pizza and taking a bite.

'Um, no, I said I'd heard of it and it's supposed to be nice – a local delicacy – but I've never tried it before.'

Simon remained expressionless as he chewed away on his first slice. Perhaps it wasn't so bad after all. He eventually swallowed and took a big gulp of his wine.

'How was it?' I asked tentatively.

'Thankfully, it doesn't taste quite as bad as it smells. But it still tastes revolting.'

'What does it taste like? Sausage?'

'Yeah, sausage. Or how I imagine a sausage made from cat food would taste.'

'Mmmm, lush.'

I took out my phone and googled L'andouille de Guémené.

'Well, what does it say? Do you think I've just got a bad batch of Lan Dooley de Gwee Meeney or whatever it's called?'

'Oh... er... I'm not sure if I should read this to you.'

'Go on. What does it say?'

'It says here that L'andouille de Guémené is made from 25 layers of pig intestine.'

'25?' said Simon, almost choking on a mouthful of wine. 'Holy shit! Because one layer of pig intestine is never enough. Well, thanks for the recommendation, George.'

'I'm really sorry. I assumed it would be nice. Do you want to swap? Or at least have half of mine?'

'No, it's fine,' he said stoically. 'The pizza underneath is quite nice. But I don't think I'll be able to eat any more of the intestine stuff.'

Local delicacies, in my experience, are always a disappointment. They rely on stupid tourists to sample them, thinking they are getting a more genuine experience. But the truth is, no local delicacy is going to be particularly special. Because if they were, their popularity would have extended beyond the small area in which they are considered a delicacy.

Still, the wine was amazing, and the double chocolate brownie and ice cream that Simon ate for pudding at least let him end the meal on a high.

Our 75 miles on Day One were tough. But to stand any chance of following the EV4 all the way to Roscoff, Day

Two was going to have to be much bigger. Probably well over 100 miles. It was a very ambitious and perhaps unlikely target, but we were going to give it a go.

TWO

We were packed up and ready to go by the time the hotel began serving breakfast at 7.00am. My cycling trousers had been annoying and uncomfortable, and I was unlikely to ever wear them again. It seemed pointless to carry them all the way back to the UK only to get rid of them when I got home, but I also couldn't bear the thought of throwing away a perfectly decent pair of trousers. So I left them (unwashed, but only worn for an hour) in the hotel room. What a treat that would be for the hotel staff.

We ate a few croissants, bread and cheese, and drank a couple of coffees in the hotel's small breakfast area. We set off half an hour before sunrise, and because of the empty roads at 7.30am on a Saturday morning, we ignored the stupid dirt track that the Google Maps lady told us to take and headed in a more direct route towards the coast, back to where we had left the Eurovelo 4 the previous evening.

'How are you feeling, Si?' I asked, as we freewheeled down a long empty road, with the sea just visible in the twilight in the distance.

'Fully refreshed and raring to go,' he said. 'Although I've

done a couple of pig intestine burps already this morning. I think it's going to be a while before I stop tasting that.'

'I'm so sorry.'

We were both feeling a little sore and achy after the previous day, but also extremely excited about spending another day cycling in France. I had spoken to Rachel and the kids the previous evening and they were all well and had a fairly quiet weekend planned. I tried to play down to Rachel how much fun we were having and instead talked mostly about Simon's pizza.

'There she is,' said Simon, as we pulled up at a junction and looked at the signpost opposite. 'Our old friend the EV4.'

This friendship was short-lived, however, because soon after joining the route, the EV4 turned off and up another stupid dirt track. We reached the harbour at Le Légué and followed the level road along either side of the estuary, with the vast sand flats below us.

The sun was low in the sky and after a freezing start (I regretted getting rid of my trousers so hastily), the day was warming up nicely. We made excellent progress during the next couple of hours; the route taking us up and over various headlands, through the picturesque ports of Binic and Saint-Quay-Portrieux. It had been about 2.5 hours since breakfast and we passed a patisserie on the edge of a town.

'Shall we stop and have a pastry or something to keep our energy levels up?' I said.

Did Not Enter

'Er, I'd like to do 25 miles before we stop. How far have we gone so far?'

'22 miles.'

'Shall we do another three and then stop for something to eat?'

'We might not pass anywhere else in three miles. This place is here. And it's open.'

'I know, but I've got it in my head that I need to do 25 miles before stopping.'

'We could buy something now, and then not eat it for another three miles?'

'Yeah, but then we would be stopping twice.'

'But what happens if there isn't anywhere else?'

'I'm sure we'll find somewhere. Is it ok if we do another three miles?'

'Yep, fine by me.'

Three miles later, we were deep in a forest, pushing our bikes along a muddy footpath, with no sign of any form of civilisation. Let alone a patisserie.

Simon had gone very quiet.

'You ok, Si?'

'Yeah, my legs have turned to jelly. We probably should have got something to eat at that last town. Sorry.'

'*You don't say!*' I muttered to myself.

Our water bottles were all empty, and I didn't even have any Hula Hoops to fall back on. It was another 13 extremely challenging miles before we found food.

'I'm really sorry for not stopping earlier,' said Simon. 'I

find long bike rides really tough – mentally and physically – and I find the only way to get through them is to break them up into chunks. I know it seems weird, but that's just how my mind works.'

This wasn't news to me at all. I already knew that Simon used various techniques to help him get through endurance events. For his two half-Ironmans he had broken down the swim section into colours of the rainbow, each colour representing a certain number of strokes. And during his marathons, he had broken the race down into eight slices of imaginary pie, each slice with a different filling.

'It's not weird at all,' I said. 'I think it's great that you use these techniques.'

'Yeah, it hasn't worked out too well today though, has it?'

'Maybe it would work better if you've either got your own food with you, or know for sure that there will be somewhere you can get food after you finish each 25-mile chunk? Rather than being deep in a forest.'

'Yeah, I know. Lesson learned.'

After refilling our water bottles and eating a couple of delicious pain au chocolats each (still not as good as the holiday park in Croyde), the jelly legs were revitalised, and we continued onward.

Despite the challenging terrain of much of the EV4 – especially on road bikes – we both really enjoyed the mystery and unpredictability of the route. You could cycle along a beautifully paved cycle path through a town centre one minute, and then be ankle-deep in mud in the middle of a forest the next.

We cycled through the village of Lézardrieux soon after midday and were both ready for lunch. There was a large boulangerie on the edge of town and we pulled up outside. A sign on the door said it was closed every day between 12 and 2pm.

'France is so weird,' said Simon. 'Why would a bakery close during lunchtime? Surely that must be their busiest time?'

'Yeah, you would have thought so. There must be another one open.'

We cycled through the town and found several more bakeries and food shops. They were all closed. Some for a two-hour lunch break, and others for the rest of the day.

To begin with, it seemed surprising (and frustrating) that a business whose sole purpose is to sell food would close during lunchtime. I then realised how wonderful it was that the French hold such importance to their mealtimes. The staff working in these establishments don't want to sacrifice that precious time during their day to cater for other people. And as this lunchtime closure is so established across much of France, people know to get their provisions beforehand. It's only needy tourists like Simon and me that have a problem with it.

We passed a sign for a big supermarket and decided we could buy stuff to make our own sandwiches instead. Only the supermarket was also closed. The French, quite rightly, hold great importance to their weekends too, and many of the supermarkets close for Saturday afternoons.

We continued along the EV4, hoping the next town might be more touristy and have some shops with anti-social opening hours. It was 2pm by the time we reached the pretty old town of Tréguier on the River Jaudy. Compared to other places we had passed through, this one was bustling with people. That still didn't mean any of the bakeries were doing business, though. Turning a corner, we came across a pizza takeaway. Thankfully, it was open.

'Hallelujah,' said Simon.

'Simon, there's this local delicacy that's supposed to be really nice. It's...'

'You can fuck right off, George,' he said. 'I'm getting a margherita.'

We ordered two margheritas and sat and ate them in the sunshine on the banks of the river.

After a leisurely lunch break, we cycled through the steep and winding old streets of Tréguier before crossing the river Guindy on an impressive old suspension bridge – the Passerelle Saint-François – and back out into the French countryside.

Simon and I became connoisseurs of French architecture during our three-day bike ride. The houses in Brittany are stunning. There's an eclectic mixture of traditional old farmhouses and manoirs, and also many new builds. But French architects and builders seem to be more adventurous than their British counterparts, and no two houses were the same. They were all exceptionally classy, as though featured in an episode of *Grand Designs*. But the most noticeable thing about these houses was that almost all of them appeared to be empty. It seems northern Brittany is a popular spot for French second-home owners (and many Brits), who live and work in Paris and other big cities and escape to the coast for the summer. In November, almost all of them were deserted.

It was looking like Lannion would be our destination for the night. I had secretly hoped we would get further, but there were a couple of factors stacked against us: we were running out of daylight, and it would be dark long before we reached Lannion; also, looking at the map, our route would not be passing through any sizable towns beyond Lannion for many miles, and we risked being stranded for the night in the middle of nowhere.

The afternoon's cycling was beautiful but demanding as we followed the pink granite coast through the popular resorts of Perros-Guirec, Tourony and Trébeurden. It was getting dark as we passed through the town of Louannec and Simon spotted a sign.

Lannion – 8 km.

'8 km? Is that all? Get in!' he said.

'Yeah, but that's if we follow the main road.'

'And I'm guessing the EV4 doesn't follow the main road?'

'No, it's a little bit further.'

'How much further?'

'It's hard to say.'

'George, roughly how much further. Please. Take a guess?'

'Err... twice as far, maybe?'

Simon sighed.

'But we don't have to do the proper route,' I said. 'We can take the main road if you'd prefer?'

'No, it's fine. Let's go.'

The EV4 route ended up being about three times the distance that the main road would have been, and we rolled into Lannion at about 8pm, both completely exhausted after 94 very difficult miles on the bike.

During those additional miles, I had come to the realisation that completing the full course of the EV4 to Roscoff the next day was not going to be possible. We still had about 80 miles of the marked route to go, which would be achievable if we had a full day's cycling. Unfortunately, our ferry departed at 3pm, with check-in required at least 45 minutes before. The EV4 followed the coastline out and around a peninsula, and if we suffered any mechanical or physical problems, getting to Roscoff in time would be unachievable. We couldn't risk missing our ferry, as there was a fairly crucial bit of information that I had not yet passed on to Simon. If we missed our ferry, the next one was not for another THREE WEEKS.

So, to ensure we made it to Roscoff in time, we would have to follow the main roads between Lannion and

Did Not Enter

Morlaix the next morning, cutting off one peninsula, before re-joining the EV4 for the last section. It would still be a ride of almost 50 miles.

There had been no phone signal for the last couple of hours before Lannion so we had been unable to pre-book any accommodation. We found a hotel in the centre of town, and although it was more expensive than we hoped, we were in no mood to look elsewhere. We stashed our bikes in the rear courtyard, went up to our room to shower and wash our cycling clothes, and then headed out to find something to eat.

'What do you fancy? Some L'andouille de Guémené?' I asked Simon.

'ANYTHING but that! I can still taste it from last night. I'm really hungry, so maybe something big and greasy.'

'Sounds perfect to me.'

The impressive River Léguer divides Lannion in two. We walked along its banks before crossing a bridge and wandered the steep back roads of what appeared to be the busy half of town. On one of the upper streets, we stumbled upon King Kebab. Now, King Kebab may not sound like the most authentic of French establishments, but it was the most popular place we had passed and there was an empty table waiting for us. Kebabs in European countries are very different to most kebabs served in Britain. They are considered proper cuisine, rather than just a drunken filler at the end of a heavy night. King Kebab had entire families sitting at the plastic tables enjoying their Saturday evening meal.

We ordered a large mixed kebab and fries each with a carafe of red wine, and we sat there in complete silence eating one of the greatest meals we had ever tasted. Although, after Simon's pizza the night before, his bar was set pretty low. We ordered another carafe of wine and continued to sit there in silence.

The family at the table next to us started chatting to us enthusiastically in French.

'Pardon. Je ne comprends pas,' I said. 'Je suis Anglais.'

They said something else in French which I think was something about how miserable Simon and I looked and why weren't we talking to each other. It's possible they were telling us something completely different, but this is how I interpreted it. I used my dreadful French and even worse miming skills to tell them we had cycled 'un très long way' and we were 'très fatigué', giving an enormous yawn and miming how I put my head on a pillow. They all started laughing and gave us a thumbs up and then looked at each other as though they had regretted beginning a conversation with two complete weirdos.

It was a long, slow walk back to our hotel, and we were so tired that I genuinely can't even remember what our hotel room looked like.

I remember the breakfast, however. Compared to the fare in Saint-Brieuc the morning before, it was a banquet. Breakfast was another part of the reason we were going to have to cut our cycling route a little short. If we had woken early and hit the road by 4am, then I confess we might have been able to cover the full 80 miles along the coast and get to our ferry in time. But staying in a hotel with breakfast included, and then not eating the breakfast, would weigh more heavily on my mind that not completing our intended route.

Simon and I made one too many trips back to the buffet, and both left the hotel feeling physically sick. We also made up a couple of cheese and ham rolls, which we folded into paper napkins and stashed into our jacket pockets with some bananas for later.

'You don't have to eat yours until we get to 25 miles,' I said.

'Don't you worry,' said Simon. 'I won't.'

As it was Sunday morning, we hoped that most of the roads between Lannion and Morlaix would be quiet. As we were temporarily off the EV4, I located which road out of town we needed to follow and used Google Maps on my phone to navigate us to it.

'I'm going to use Google's cycling navigation again,' I said tentatively.

'Really? Remember what happened last time? We ended up on that stupidly hilly dirt track.'

'I know, but this time it will be different. We were still in the suburbs then. Now we are in the middle of a big city. There can't possibly be any dirt tracks. It makes sense to use the most cycle-friendly route out of the town, doesn't it?'

'I guess so,' said Simon, not looking convinced.

We heaved our overly full bellies onto our bikes and began cycling in the direction instructed by my phone. We turned down towards the river and followed a nice smooth section of quiet road with beautiful views across the water.

'This is ace!' I said.

The Google Maps lady then directed us into the hospital car park.

'Are you sure this is right, George?'

'That's what she's saying. It must be a shortcut to a cycle path or another road.'

We followed the navigation all the way around the outside of the hospital, to the far end of the car park where the tarmac ended.

'See, I told you we should have ignored the Google Maps lady. How has it led us to a dead end in a hospital car park?'

'She doesn't think this is a dead end. She says we should keep going.'

'Keep going? Where?'

'That way,' I said, pointing to the thick woodland that lined one edge of the car park.

'Ha, yeah right.'

'That's what she says. Look!' I said, showing Simon my phone.

'Well, the Google Maps lady is clearly mental. There is no route there.'

I pedalled forwards up to the very edge of the empty car

park. Just on the other side of the grass verge, there was an opening between the trees with a narrow pathway descending steeply into the woods.

'Come and look, it looks like there is a route.'

Simon shuffled forwards and brought his bike alongside mine.

'You've got to be fucking kidding me. That's not a cycle path.'

'No. But maybe it's just a really short section that links up to a road just through the woods?'

'You're going to make us go that way, aren't you?'

'I'm just doing what she says.'

Simon gave a heavy sigh.

The path was too steep, and the fallen leaves piled too deep for us to cycle, so we wheeled our bikes down into the forest, hoping we would soon meet a road. But we didn't. The path became more and more overgrown the further we continued, and at one point we had to lift our bikes over a couple of fallen trees.

'George, I think perhaps we should ignore the Google Maps lady from now on. Or at least her cycling option.'

'I think you're right.'

After about half a mile, the trees thinned up ahead, and the path opened out onto a bumpy farm track which we followed for another half mile before eventually reaching a road.

'See, never in doubt!' I said. 'I bet that was a massive shortcut.'

'Er, we left the hotel 45 minutes ago, we've travelled two miles, and I can still see Lannion just there.'

I followed Simon's gaze along a perfectly flat and smooth tarmac road, with no cars in either direction. The suburbs of Lannion were just there, a couple of minutes away by bike.

'Ok, maybe it wasn't a shortcut. But we wouldn't have got to see that lovely forest if we had followed the road.'

Once on the main road, it was much easier going and we made it to Saint-Michel-en-Grève, where the road hugged the coast for a couple of miles before a series of long climbs outside Morlaix. Compared to the gravel and dirt tracks we had encountered since the start of our trip, these hills felt easy. There was obviously more traffic on the main roads than we had been used to, but as it was Sunday morning, they were still relatively quiet.

We stopped briefly in Morlaix where we would re-join our old friend the EV4. Simon took off his helmet and I worried briefly that he was going to lie down for nap.

'I think we better get a move on,' I said. 'We don't want to miss the ferry.'

'Ah, I won't be long,' he said. 'Anyway, it wouldn't be the end of the world if we missed the ferry, would it? I'd be well up for staying another night in France and getting tomorrow's one instead.'

'Um... there isn't a ferry tomorrow.'

'Tuesday then? Even better. I'm sure I could get a couple more days off work.'

Did Not Enter

'There isn't one on Tuesday either. If we miss this ferry, the next one isn't for... er... three weeks.'

'THREE WEEKS?' he shouted, sitting bolt upright. 'Are you serious?'

'Yes. I think the ferry company take their winter break in November.'

'Holy shit! Why didn't you tell me? We had better get a move on.'

'I was worried it would stress you out.'

The EV4 predictably took us off-road into the middle of nowhere within minutes of our reintroduction. On these sections, far from any main road, I had slight panics about having some sort of catastrophic bike malfunction. We had very basic bike provisions: a couple of inner tubes, a pump and a multi-tool. But if one of our tyres split, a chain broke, wheel buckled, or something else serious, we were fucked. The probability of any one of these mechanical breakdowns occurring was dramatically increased because of our bikes being so unsuitable to the terrain. Every rut, every pothole, every rock, every loose stone, and the build-up of mud and dust threatened to bring our ride to an abrupt end. If it did, we would have to walk to the nearest road and try to phone for a taxi. But out in the middle of nowhere, we were potentially a long way from help, and our chances of missing the ferry became very real. I tried to block these thoughts from my mind and certainly didn't voice them to Simon.

We reached the outskirts of Saint-Pol-de-Léon just after 1pm, which left us with an hour to cover the final five miles to Roscoff. I breathed a sigh of relief. Surely nothing could stop us now.

We were cycling along a lovely stretch of quiet road, alongside the old stonewall that borders the grounds of Château de Kernévez. We turned a corner to head through the town centre and were greeted with a fence across the road. Police officers carrying semi-automatic weapons stood guard. We slammed on the brakes.

It appeared to be the finish line of a running event. Metal barriers lined the road on either side, and a large scaffolding construction and timing clock mounted to it arched over the finish line. But apart from the armed guards, there was nobody else around.

'Which way do we go now?' asked Simon.

'Up that way, according to my watch.'

'Well, it looks like that way is closed. We will have to find another way, I guess.'

'But the other way might be much longer. There's nobody here. Surely they will let us through.'

'Let's just find a different route, George.'

'But this is the way the EV4 goes.'

Simon rolled his eyes.

'I'll go and speak to them,' I said.

I wheeled my bike up to one of the stern-looking gendarmes.

'Bonjour. Est possible on bicyclette?' I said, pointing up

Did Not Enter

the road.

'Non. Ferme,' he said.

I pulled out my phone and showed him that our route went that way.

'Ferme,' he said again, more sternly this time.

'George, I think we should leave it,' called Simon.

'But that's our route!'

'Forget our route. It doesn't matter.'

'But we are so close!'

'George!'

I tried one last time.

'Excusez moi. Nous traverser dans la grass?' I asked, pointing to the grass verge on the other side of the barriers.

The police officer looked over his shoulder to where I was pointing and then at his colleague next to him. The other police officer shrugged his shoulders.

'D'accord. Vit!'

'Merci monsieur.'

'What did he say?' asked Simon when I beckoned him over.

'He said we can walk on the grass verge, but we have to be quick.'

We carried our bikes across the grass on the other side of the barrier for about 100 metres before passing more armed guards at the other end and mounting our bikes again. I have no idea why an empty finishing chute was being so heavily guarded by armed police, but we didn't want to question it.

Although the direct road route from Saint-Pol-de-Léon to Roscoff is only about three miles, the EV4 still had a few last surprises for us. From Saint-Pol-de-Léon, we followed a road out of town, and we came across a drinks station set up for the run. We chatted in our awful French to a marshal who told us it was the annual Saint Pol – Morlaix half-marathon, which takes place, unsurprisingly, between the towns of Saint Pol and Morlaix. The start time wasn't until 1.40pm, which is very civilised and French compared to the early start of most British races, and they did not expect the first runners through for a couple more hours.

'Merci monsieur. Au revoir,' I said, as we cycled away from him, heading towards an EV4 sign away from the main road.

'NON! NON! NON!' he shouted, chasing after us.

What had we done wrong now? This man didn't carry a machine gun but seemed equally adamant that we shouldn't go any further.

'Oui,' I said, pointing to the sign. 'Eurovelo 4.'

'Non,' he said. 'Roscoff? Continuez tout droit, tournez à droite...', he began, pointing us in a different direction.

'Why can't we go down here?' asked Simon.

'I'm not sure. Surely the runners won't be coming up this way?'

I tried asking the man and he shook his head. This time he pointed to our bikes and told us they weren't suitable and that the track was very bad, and we definitely wouldn't be able to do it on our road bikes.

'Ahhh, merci. It's ok. We'll be fine,' I said.

'Non, non, non!' he said, smiling this time.

'Oui, oui, oui,' I said. I wanted to tell him about all the other dirt tracks we'd cycled on and the forests we had found ourselves in, but my French didn't stretch that far.

The man just stood there and shook his head, as we politely ignored him and pedalled off along the EV4. Within the first 100 metres, the track turned deeply rutted and uneven. It would have been a challenge on a mountain bike, but on a road bike it was almost impossible to cycle on. But we couldn't turn back now after being so insistent that we would be fine. I looked back over my shoulder and could still see him standing watching us.

'Is he still there?' asked Simon, as he jolted in and out of a series of deep potholes.

'Yep. Just keep pedalling. We will soon be out of sight.'

Once over the cusp of the hill, we dismounted our bikes and pushed them for a while until the track surface became a little more bearable. We eventually emerged from the dirt track onto a smooth main road, and I realised we were now safely within touching distance of Roscoff. I recognised this section of road from our holidays in France and knew it was only a couple of miles to the ferry port. If we had any bike problems here, we could walk and still get to the ferry in time.

'Ah, tarmac, how I've missed you,' said Simon. 'Do we

just follow this road all the way to the ferry port?'

'Er, no. Not according to that EV4 sign. It wants us to go that way,' I said, pointing in the opposite direction to Roscoff.

'But the road sign says Roscoff is that way.'

'I know, maybe we only go that way for a little bit.'

'Well, I know there's no point trying to change your mind.'

'I'm just doing what the route tells us.'

We turned right and then immediately took a tight left corner, back towards Roscoff, but on a path rather than the road. This path then went over a small footbridge and across a section of beach that would have been mostly underwater at high tide. From there to Roscoff, we meandered through tiny French villages and beautiful countryside, before emerging within sight of the ferry port.

'See, that was so much better than the main road, wasn't it?' I said, as we freewheeled down to passport control.

'Yeah, it was really nice. Imagine where the Google Maps lady would have taken us.'

We made it to Roscoff with an hour to spare before our ferry departed.

'We did it!' I said, giving Simon a big sweaty hug.

'Awesome, well done, buddy. Thanks for suggesting this trip. It was brilliant. How far did we go today?'

I checked my watch.

'45 miles. That's 213 miles in two-and-a-half days. I think that's pretty bloody good over that terrain.'

'I'm well chuffed with that.'

'Me too.'

They allowed Simon and me onto the ferry before any of the cars or foot passengers, which meant we had a pick of the seats. We chose two at the front of the boat, with panoramic views of the English Channel, I mean la Manche, in front of us. Strangely, the sight of two sweaty, lycra-clad cyclists didn't encourage anyone to come and sit next to us.

It was a truly memorable trip. The route was much harder than I expected, but that was only because of our choice of bikes. Cycling in France had been a joy. The scenery, the people, the food (except the 25-intestine sausage), the company, and the peace and quiet all made for a fantastic three days.

We felt very lucky to have taken advantage of the one and only ferry crossing to Saint-Malo. Having a designated A to B route gave us a purpose, and the looming threat of missing the last ferry of the season gave the trip an extra level of excitement. It had been an adventure that I know would have made Doug smile.

I had been a little disappointed when I realised we would not be able to cycle the full section of the EV4, and if our sole mission was to cycle along the EV4, then by that definition we would both be marked down as DNF. But the goal had always been to cycle from Saint-Malo to Roscoff. My original message to Simon had stated the contingency plan of using the road if the marked route was not achievable. And having that massive hotel breakfast had made the longer route unachievable. The missing section of the EV4 between Lannion and Morlaix now gave me an incentive to return to France one day to finish what we missed. Or maybe one day I could follow it all the way to Kiev?

THREE

In early December, we took the kids out of school for the day and drove up to Northampton for Doug's funeral. It was a very small gathering of about a dozen people at a local church. Doug had no family and having been a full-time carer for his wife Christine, had few close friends. We were really pleased we had made the journey.

From the church, we drove to the graveyard in another part of town. As they lowered the coffin into the ground and said a few prayers, it began to pour with rain. Leo asked if he could go back to the van which was parked up close by. I handed Leo (aged 8) the keys and somehow between leaving the grave and getting to the van, he managed to set the alarm off with the key fob. It was several minutes before we could turn it off, and in a strange way it provided some much-needed light relief to the sombre occasion. Doug would have found it very amusing.

Directly after the funeral, we called into the care home to visit Doug's wife Christine who could not attend, before beginning the long drive back to Devon.

Rachel sat in the passenger seat, scrolling through her

phone.

'Aw, this one is adorable,' she said.

'What are you looking at?'

'Oh, just looking at puppies.'

'Puppies? Really? I thought we agreed we would start looking properly sometime after Christmas?'

'I know, I'm just looking. Look at that face though!'

She held up her phone and showed me a picture of a small hairy black and white puppy. It did look very cute. Although, it's not often you see a really ugly puppy.

'Can we see?' said Leo from the back seat.

Rachel passed her phone back, and all three children spent the next few minutes cooing over it.

'Can we get it, Mummy? Please, it's SOOO cute,' said Kitty (aged 7).

'No, I don't think so,' said Rachel. 'It's probably been reserved already.'

'Where is it?' I asked.

'Devon. About half an hour from home, I think. Why? Are you tempted to go and see it?'

'I don't know. Maybe.'

'I'm working all week and we've got things on most evenings so I don't know when we would get to see it.'

'We could call in on the way home today,' I whispered.

'Really? We probably won't be there until about eight or nine o'clock.'

'What was that?' said Layla (aged 11) with her bat-like hearing. 'Are we going to see the puppy tonight?'

'Daddy and I are just discussing it,' said Rachel. 'We don't even know if it's still available.'

'Give them a call,' I said.

Rachel phoned the number and spoke to the owners. Two hours later, we had been to visit and paid a deposit.

Turning up to view a puppy with three excitable children, and an even more excited wife, was always going to end with us getting one. The puppy's mum was a working border collie, and his dad a weird-looking miniature poodle, so he was a Bordoodle or a Colliepoo. Although the puppies would be ready a week before Christmas, the breeders were being responsible and were not allowing any of them to be collected until after Christmas to discourage any impulse Christmas present purchases.

Standing there still wearing our funeral attire, you couldn't get much more impulsive than we had been. But getting a dog had been on the cards for a long time. And it's probably something I would have just kept putting off for no real reason. There was something serendipitous about buying a dog on the way home from a funeral. You know, the circle of life, and all that.

I even suggested naming the puppy Doug, but Rachel and the kids had decided on a name long before they had even started looking at dogs. He was going to be called Ludo, named after the big hairy monster in the film *Labyrinth*. It suited him perfectly.

It was a long four-week wait until we could collect

Ludo. Christmas provided a much-needed distraction and there was plenty going on with school plays, Christmas fairs, and a big family Christmas to keep our minds from being exclusively occupied with puppy thoughts. We squeezed in a second visit to see Ludo just before Christmas.

Between Christmas and New Year, we drove back to Northampton again to spend a couple of days with Rachel's family and meet up with old friends (including my friend Damo, who claims his grandma invented banoffee pie). Then on New Year's Eve, we went to collect Ludo.

FOUR

I am not a big fan of New Year's resolutions; especially ones that involve giving up something you like – sugar, alcohol, chocolate. January can be a bit of a shit and depressing month, and it seems cruel to make the start of the year even tougher by depriving yourself of these pleasures. Also, January is a time of the year when your house is usually overflowing with snacks, chocolates and alcohol, left over from the festive period.

But I like the satisfaction of creating self-imposed challenges and trying to stick to them. So rather than have a new year's resolution that stopped me doing something, I prefer resolutions that add something instead.

So I set myself a challenge of running 10k every day in January. It was not a challenge I planned in advance. Getting Ludo on December 31st meant we had a quiet evening at home, so I woke up on New Year's Day without the usual raging hangover, full of excitement and enthusiasm for the year ahead, which is usually clouded by a throbbing headache. And the upcoming year was made even more exciting because of our family's recent addition.

I went out for a run to capitalise on my smugness, and when I returned home feeling awesome, the 10k a day idea sprang to mind.

It was not until a year later that I realised that running every day in January is now a recognised movement. I'm not claiming I pioneered it. RED January (Run Every Day) was founded in 2016 by Hannah Beecham, with the aim to encourage people to get active each day in January to support their own mental health.

To make things a little more exciting and challenging, I decided that each 10k run had to be a different route. I had got into the habit of sticking to a small handful of tried and tested run routes, which were mostly decided on because they had the fewest number of severe hills. But there was so much of the local area I was unfamiliar with, and so many more potential roads and trails to follow.

At some point each day throughout January, I went for a 10k run. Some routes were planned beforehand, and others I just winged when I was out and about. For a few of the runs, I drove to a beach to run along the coast path, but the vast majority were from my front door. I took every bridleway, every footpath, every road and green lane in the local area, many of which I didn't even know existed. Towards the end of the month, when I was low on ideas, I did a couple of routes I had done earlier in the month but in reverse. In the opposite direction, I mean, not running backwards.

But what was the point? Why would I choose to punish

myself in this way (as Layla kept asking)? Why is this better than giving up chocolate or alcohol? It was not just a means to improve my fitness, it was because the rewards I was offering myself made it more than worthwhile. I would not stop drinking or eating unhealthily during January. In fact, I planned to drink most nights in celebration, and slowly work my way through all the cheese and chocolate we had accumulated over Christmas, safe in the knowledge that running 10k a day should still leave me with a net health gain at the end of the month. When I first heard about RED January, I didn't pick up on the 'Run Every Day' acronym, and genuinely thought it was a parody opposition to Dry January, instead encouraging people to drink red wine every day during the month. So that's pretty much what I did. I celebrated Red RED January and had the best Januarys ever.

It wasn't easy. I had never done many runs on consecutive days before, and after the first week of running every day, my body felt pretty broken. But it soon adapted as I went along, and after about ten days there were no ongoing aches and pains and my body seemed to have accepted that running every day was the new normal.

There were a couple of occasions early on in the month when my challenge nearly came to an end. During my bike ride with Simon in Brittany, I had started to experience painful toothache. I went to the dentist when I got home and was told that it would hopefully settle down. It continued to cause problems over Christmas, and I planned to leave it another week and then go back to the dentist if it hadn't improved. Then one day, in the first week of January, I was sitting at home watching television when I heard a slight cracking sound from my mouth. I put my finger into the back of my mouth and discovered my rear molar had split in half. I couldn't understand how a tooth that I was told had been healthy could have split in half, especially considering I wasn't even eating or chewing at the time. Strangely, my toothache seemed to have disappeared. But having a tooth that was split in half was unlikely to be a good thing.

I phoned the dentist the next morning and they squeezed me in as an emergency appointment. She did an x-ray and discovered the cause of the split molar was an impacted wisdom tooth. My wisdom tooth was growing sideways towards the front of my mouth, right into the path of the molar. Pressure on the nerve roots had caused the pain, and the wisdom tooth eventually won the turf war by splitting the molar in half.

'Can it be glued back together?' I asked, as both sections were still embedded in my gum.

'No, not really. It could get infected and would only split again if the wisdom tooth keeps growing into it. The molar has to go, I'm afraid. It's the back one, so it's not too important.'

'Ok. Is it difficult to remove? Will it be painful?'

'No, it shouldn't be too bad. I'll give you a small injection which will numb your face for a while and then

Did Not Enter

we can do the extraction.'

I winced as she stuck the needle into my gums and then gave the tooth a gentle wiggle. Each half came out intact in her fingers.

'Oh, I didn't need to give you that injection after all. It's out already without having to do the extraction.'

'Wow, thank you. That didn't hurt at all. Is that awful smell coming from my mouth?'

'Yes, the tooth hole is full of pus. No wonder it was causing you so much pain. I'll give it a good clean out now.'

A few minutes later, when the revolting taste from my mouth had finally disappeared, she removed her visor.

'You're all good to go. Just take it easy for a day or two. No alcohol after your anaesthetic, and you don't want to do anything too strenuous because you could disturb the clot that has formed in the hole. That will help it seal over properly.'

'Ok, thanks very much for your help.'

It wasn't until I got home that I remembered my 10k challenge. If I was heeding the dentist's advice, then a run was completely out of the question. But it was only Day 6 of the challenge, and that would be a pretty pathetic way to fail. It wasn't worth the risk, though, so I took the dentist's advice, had some soup for dinner, and then took it easy in front of the TV with my numb face.

Later that evening, I had a nagging feeling of failure. I had only had a tooth removed. It's not like I'd had major surgery. I called Simon and asked if he fancied going for a late night, very slow 10k run/walk. He was well up for the idea and my streak was able to continue. I did gallantly abstain from the red wine that night, though.

On another occasion, Layla, Leo and Kitty were off school because of an inset day. Rachel works as a teacher so had to attend. Despite their protests, I took the kids on a seven-mile walk that I had been wanting to do for a while. Ludo hadn't yet had all of his vaccinations, so was not allowed out in public, and was also too young to go on such a long walk.

By the time we made it back to the car, the four of us were suitably tired. Layla, Leo and Kitty all enjoyed it a lot more than they expected to, and it made me very excited about all the walking we would get to do with Ludo. On the drive home, I remembered my 10k a day challenge. I had just walked more than 10k. *Surely that counts?*

'No, of course it doesn't count!' said Layla. 'You'll have to go and run 10k when we get home.'

'I think it counts,' said Leo.

'Me too,' said Kitty.

'You're clearly cheating,' said Layla.

'Cheating? I'm not exactly cheating, am I? I mean, I have done 10k today. In fact, seven miles is more than 10k.'

'But you didn't run it, did you?'

'Well, no. But my challenge was just 10k every day. I didn't say it had to be running, did I?'

'Maybe not, but you know that's what you meant.'

Did Not Enter

Part of me agreed with Layla. I was using the walk as a substitute for heading out for a run. The other part of me couldn't understand why Layla was being such a stickler for the rules. I have no idea where she gets it from.

When Rachel got home, she agreed that my walk should count. I think perhaps she only said that so that I didn't disappear out and leave her to sort dinner for everyone. I texted Simon, who could act as an impartial adjudicator. He replied:

'The walk totally counts. I am with the Mahood majority. Cast aside any non-believers.'

I didn't go out again that day and Layla still claims I failed.

The rest of the month was a great success, and I ended the month much fitter (and fatter) than I had started. I hope to repeat Red RED January every year.

FIVE

Puppy training had been going pretty well. Things hadn't got off to the best start when we first collected Ludo. He was sick in the car on the way home, all over himself and the blanket they had given us with his mother's scent on. We gave him a quick bath when we got home and then he rolled in a fox poo in the garden, so had his second bath of the day in the space of a couple of hours. We did momentarily wonder what we had got ourselves into.

Ludo had his fair share of accidents on the carpet and kitchen floor in the first few days, but he was soon able to let us know when he needed to go outside. I was usually last to bed and tasked with getting him to have one last visit to the garden before I went upstairs. This was always the most tedious – but impossibly amusing – part of the day. After an exhausting day doing what puppies do, Ludo would be totally dead to the world on the lounge floor or more likely the sofa (keeping him off the sofa lasted less than 12 hours). I would have to either usher or carry him outside where he would stand in the cold and stare at me, his eyes barely open, while I made animated noises to get him to go to the toilet. After about five minutes of standing there, he would invariably lie down on the cold wet grass and go back to sleep, and I would have to nudge him and try to get him to stand up. Eventually he would start sniffing around the garden for a suitable place to go, and we would both be able to return to the warmth of the house.

There are three other dogs on the farm where we live: two working border collies, and one pet labrador. All are free range most of the day. From the moment Ludo arrived, the other three dogs would appear on top of our garden wall several times during the day to check out the new kid on the block. For the first few days, the three of them stayed on the wall, with Ludo bouncing up from below, desperate to play but too small to climb. Once they realised that Ludo wasn't a threat, the three dogs all ventured down from the wall to our garden and have been best friends ever since.

Layla, Leo, and Kitty loved having a dog, and particularly enjoyed those first few weeks when he was mostly housebound. They then enjoyed the novelty of going out on walks and taking him to the beach. But the dog walking novelty soon wore off when they realised this was how we would spend our weekends from now on.

For the first few years after moving to Devon, we had family membership at a local theme park called Woodlands, and on cold and wet winter weekends we often ended up in their indoor soft play area. After slightly outgrowing Woodlands, we didn't renew our membership and instead spent many wet weekends at the local swimming pool (where we also had family membership) to experience the trauma of their Family Float Session. But since training for my double-dart 10k, I had not been back to the swimming pool. And as Layla, Leo and Kitty had each progressed further in their swimming lessons than I had as a child, we ended our leisure centre membership, too.

Now our cold and wet winter weekends were spent walking Ludo. This prospect was not too appealing for Layla, Leo and Kitty, and they kicked up a protest every single time. But Rachel and I were fully aware of the mental and physical boost we would all get from being outside, whatever the weather. And having Ludo meant it was no longer up for discussion.

SIX

Since having my back problems, I occasionally dabbled with a bit of yoga. Rachel and I attended one yoga class together, but all of my other experiments had been via YouTube. I had attempted a couple of different 30-day yoga challenges, but each time failed before reaching the halfway point of the month. I knew it would be beneficial to me, as my overall flexibility was extremely poor. For as long as I can remember, I have not been able to touch my toes. And despite feeling fairly fit and healthy, my toes now seemed further away than ever before.

As well as my 10k per day challenge, this January I decided to do another 30-day yoga challenge. But this time I was determined to make sure I could see it through to the end of the month.

Yogi Adriene has several 30-day YouTube challenges, and the daily videos in each course range from about 15 minutes up to about 50. I confess that my level of enjoyment seemed to be inversely proportional to their length. Not because I found the yoga boring, but because

I found it so hard. I thought yoga was supposed to be easy. *If old grannies can do it, then surely I can too?* It surprised me not only how difficult some of it was, but also how painful. I had no idea it was possible to inflict so much pain on myself in my own living room.

I stuck with it, though, and became very disciplined with my daily practice. Some mornings I would do it as soon as I woke up, and other days I would squeeze it in at random times of the day. Occasionally, I would remember my daily challenge late into the evening and would then have to interrupt my TV viewing for an impromptu yoga session. One night, midway through January, I remembered my yoga as I was going to bed at about 11.40pm. I had already consumed an entire bottle of red wine and even standing tall in 'mountain pose' was problematic. Anything involving any semblance of balance was almost impossible, but I got through the session and maintained my streak.

I tried several times to get Rachel to join me.

'No thanks. I can already touch my toes,' she said.

'It's not about touching your toes.'

'Well, I don't think yoga is for me. It's a bit slow and boring.'

'It can be. But it's really difficult yet relaxing at the same time. I think you would like it.'

She wasn't convinced and chose to sit and laugh at me from the sofa instead.

January 31st arrived, and I had not missed a single day. My challenge was complete, and after my failed attempts in previous years, I was extremely proud of finishing the month. I still couldn't touch my toes, but I definitely felt better than I had at the beginning of the month. And despite it being difficult, and sometimes slow and boring, I also didn't want it to end. So, I started on a different month-long challenge and completed a session every single day in February too.

Midway through February, not only was I finding many of the poses easier than I had done at the start of January, but I was also enjoying – and sometimes even looking forward to – my daily yoga session. Not just because of the physical benefit it was giving me, but for that brief period of peace and relaxation during the day. There were some days when it felt like a chore, but I was committed to the challenge and enjoyed the satisfaction of completing my daily task.

February ended and again I wasn't ready to quit, so I embarked on another 30-day yoga challenge through the month of March. Beginning a different course each time made it feel like I was moving forward, rather than starting again from scratch each time. It now felt cemented as a daily habit, and it was difficult to imagine yoga not being a part of my life.

SEVEN

Rachel had shown no interest in my plans to cycle through Brittany in November. She thought it would be cold, wet and miserable, and was more than happy to see the back of me for three days while I went to France with Simon. But after hearing all about the trip, seeing the photos of the beautiful beaches and glorious blue sky, she was very envious of our adventure and said she wished she had agreed to come with me.

So, instead of the now traditional place in a European marathon as a Christmas present for Rachel, I booked us a ferry crossing to France in the middle of March. We would take our bikes over on the night ferry and spend two full days cycling around Brittany before catching another night ferry home. I had arranged for my parents to look after the kids, and we were all set.

When I gave Rachel the envelope with a makeshift 'voucher' inside for Christmas, she wasn't as excited as I hoped. She put on a fake smile, but I could tell she was disappointed. I broached the subject later that night.

'Do you not like the idea of cycling in France?'

'Yes... I do,' she said hesitantly.

'But?'

'But what?'

'You don't seem very excited.'

'I am... it's just... I don't know.'

'You said you thought my trip with Simon sounded brilliant.'

'I know. It did. But that didn't necessarily mean that I wanted to do it.'

'You said you did.'

'Did I?'

'Yes. Several times.'

'Oh, I guess I meant your trip sounded really fun... for you and Simon.'

'We'll have a great time. It will be fun.'

'I'm sure it will. Thank you,' she said, but she didn't sound convinced.

'Would you have preferred another marathon somewhere?'

'No... well... maybe.'

'I'm sorry. I did look, but I couldn't find any suitable events that matched up with when Mum and Dad were free to have the kids. And the flights were all so expensive and were all at the wrong airports.'

'It's honestly fine. France will be great!'

In the few months following Christmas, our trip to Brittany was rarely mentioned. This meant that Rachel was either trying not to think about it or was hoping it would never happen. In the week before we were due to leave, various things came up that threatened to derail our plans completely. Rachel injured her foot and was struggling to run or cycle; then the kids took it in turns to be ill; and then Storm Gareth descended on Britain's shores, cancelling dozens of ferries the week before our trip. Rachel seemed to relax, thinking it was unlikely our ferry crossing would go ahead. *I mean, who would go on a cycling holiday during a severe storm?* But the day before we were due to leave, the children all felt better, Rachel's foot didn't feel as bad, and despite the predicted continuation of Storm Gareth over the weekend, our ferry was scheduled to go ahead as planned.

'We really don't have to go if you don't want to,' I said on the day of our ferry.

'It's fine. They wouldn't run the ferry tonight if it's not safe, would they?'

'No, of course not. It will be fine. It will be fun.'

'Hmmph.'

'It will be.'

'George, I'm not sure how cycling in 50mph wind and heavy rain is going to be fun,' said Rachel, sounding quite angry for the first time.

Rachel had been checking the weather obsessively for the previous week, presumably hoping that the wind was going to pick up enough for our ferry crossing to be cancelled.

'Does it really say 50mph wind?' I said.

'Yes.'

'Well, if the weather is terrible when we get there, we can just stay in Roscoff.'

'Two days at the ferry port? Woo hoo!'

'No, not at the ferry port. At a hotel.'

I had not yet booked any accommodation for our night in France. I had hoped to cycle 40 or 50 miles down the coast, find somewhere to stay the night, and then cycle back on the second day. But because of the weather, I knew our plans may change so had waited before committing. This lack of any sort of plan was adding to Rachel's anxiety.

Another reason for Rachel's reticence about our trip to France was her 40th birthday, which was lurking a few days away. Turning 40 had been a weight on Rachel's mind for a while, and as the day got closer, her fear of facing it increased. She wanted to do anything possible to avoid having any sort of organised celebration, but also wanted to mark her birthday in some way. I had thought that cycling in France might be the perfect way to both mark it and avoid celebrating it, but a couple of days of being beaten around by Storm Gareth was apparently not what she had envisaged.

We parked the van at the ferry port in Plymouth with the rain lashing down, and a wild wind all around. We proceeded through passport control, wheeling our bikes with a small backpack each and a carrier bag containing wine, crisps and chocolate for our night on the ferry.

'I'm sorry, Sir, I'm going to have to confiscate these,'

said a stern-looking customs official, doing a spot check of our bags before boarding.

'Really? Are we not allowed to take our own food and drink onto the ferry? Sorry, I didn't realise.'

'Of course you are,' he said. 'I'm only kidding. I just wanted them for myself. Have a great trip, guys!'

Rachel smiled for the first time in a while.

Once on-board, I knew we were at least going to France. Whether we would get any cycling done was still unknown, but we would be in France for two days, whatever happened. Unless of course the boat sank. But I didn't mention that to Rachel.

Still safely moored in Plymouth dock, the ferry was perfectly still, so we sat in the lounge area, and I opened the wine and crisps. While Rachel nipped off to the toilet, I pulled out my phone and booked us a room at the posh-looking Brittany & Spa Hotel, which was less than half a mile from Roscoff's ferry port. If the weather was too bad when we arrived in France the following morning, we would have 48 hours in a lovely hotel in Roscoff, which sounded incredibly tempting.

When I told Rachel the news, her entire mood changed completely. Gone was the feeling of unease and uncertainty, and it was replaced by a glimmer of optimism and excitement.

It didn't last.

The ferry crossing was the worst we had ever experienced, and the boat rocked violently from side to side all night. We had to use the belts in our bunk beds to strap ourselves in. The wine, crisps and chocolate we had consumed before bed no longer felt like such a great idea, and Rachel's enthusiasm for our French adventure was once again on a rapid downward spiral.

It was the middle of March, and I had been continuing my daily yoga challenge. As the ferry neared Roscoff the following morning, Rachel woke to the sight of me trying to perform Downward Facing Dog in the cramped cabin room as the boat continued listing manically. She burst out laughing, which at least ensured our time in France got off to a positive start.

We filled up a tray of breakfast each from the canteen and comically walked to a table like we were taking part in a circus act. But as we finished our coffees and the ferry came into the dock in Roscoff, the sea calmed slightly, and we felt a little more human. The sky was heavily overcast, but there was no sign of the forecast rain.

Rachel and I were first off the ferry and through passport control by 8.15am. We had not even discussed our cycling plans or what or where we were going. I didn't want to put any pressure on Rachel to cycle anywhere at all if she didn't fancy it, so we turned right and headed towards the hotel.

'Check-in is not until 2pm, but we could see if they will let us check in early,' I said.

'I think we should do some cycling. That is what we

came here for.'

'I know, but that was before Storm Gareth came. I honestly don't mind if you want to just spend the day in the hotel and spa instead.'

'The spa will still be there later. Let's do some cycling and see how it goes.'

'Ok. Are you sure?'

'I'm sure. Where shall we go?'

I had cycled the roads east from Roscoff during my ride with Simon in November the previous year. I had never been west.

'Shall we just head down the coast that way and see what it's like?'

'Sounds good.'

'I think the wind will be against us most of the way, but then we should have a tail wind all the way back.'

Most visitors to Roscoff see nothing but the ferry port. On our annual holidays to France over the previous four years, that was all we had seen, too. But Roscoff is a beautiful town with a fascinating history, and it has played an important part in France's relationship with the UK. The stereotype of French men riding bikes with onions hanging from their handlebars originates in Roscoff. As early as 1828, Bretons – often dressed in the traditional striped shirt and beret – found a market for their produce on the other side of the Channel (sorry, la Manche), and would cycle door-to-door in the south west of England and

Wales selling their popular pink onions. By the 1920s they numbered in the thousands and were a popular sight on streets across Britain. An unusual proportion of them were named Jean – or at least claimed to be – so the nickname Onion Johnnies became synonymous with these French salesmen.

Unlike my Brittany trip with Simon, Rachel and I had no time constraints to get to a certain point or cover a certain number of miles. I had no vibrating watch telling me we had gone wrong, no GPS line to follow, and no annoying Google Maps lady leading us down ridiculous tracks. We just kept the sea on our right and stayed as close to the coast as possible. On many occasions, we took a right turn down a quiet lane only for it to end at a beautiful, secluded beach with bright white sand and spectacular rock formations. Each beach was deserted, as it was a cold and windy Friday morning in March, and not exactly prime holiday season. There was a strong headwind, and it was tough going, but Rachel seemed to enjoy herself much more than I (and I think she) anticipated. She was wearing a thin windproof cycling jacket and was struggling with the cold. I had a thicker high-vis coat on, so after a few miles we swapped, and despite Rachel's jacket being a little figure-hugging on me, it was more than enough to keep me warm.

By mid-morning, we were both craving a hot drink and something to eat. The villages we passed through were tiny, and none of them had shops or cafes. In some villages, the local boulangeries have been replaced by baguette vending machines. Their introduction and rapid spread across France has divided opinion. Some think they are the biggest travesty to hit the modern world. Others consider them to be the best thing since... er... sliced bread.

At a road junction on the outskirts of Sibiril, we passed the only open establishment we had seen in over an hour. It was a biker bar and tobacconist and was possibly the most random thing I have seen in rural France. It was open and there was a sign advertising coffee, so we propped our bikes outside and entered.

I had expectations of passing through its doors in my bicycle helmet and lycra to be greeted by the glare of hordes of leather clad bikers. I need not have worried. It was 10.30am and the place was empty. I ordered two coffees and we took a seat at the American-style diner seats in the corner. There was no food on offer, but the coffees did the job, and we ordered two more, partly to keep us warm and delay going back outside, but mostly because they were each served with a tiny little biscuit.

'How far have we cycled so far?' asked Rachel.

'Eleven miles. Shall we turn back? We could be back in Roscoff in time for lunch.'

'I think we should do twenty.'

'Twenty? Even if we cycle back to Roscoff from here, we will have done 22.'

'No, I mean 20 before turning back. Then I can do 40

for my 40th.'

'Are you serious? You want to do another nine miles in this wind?'

'Yes, why not? I'm enjoying it. And you said we will have the wind behind us the whole way back.'

'That's true. Well, ok then, 40 miles sounds great to me.'

The brief rest, the coffee and the biscuits had given us both a much-needed boost to both our energy levels and morale, and we made good progress along the coast. After 18 miles we parked up our bikes alongside Plage de La Grenouillère in Cléder and sat on the beach for another break.

'Have you still got the rest of that wine from last night?' asked Rachel.

'Yes, why?'

'Shall we have it now?'

'I like your style!'

Squashed into my small rucksack, I had brought the bottle of red wine from the ferry which was still about a third full. We sat on a rock by the beach and swigged it from a bottle.

'So, are you having fun?' I asked tentatively.

'I might be. A little,' smiled Rachel.

'Just a little?'

'Ok, a lot. You were right. I'm having a really lovely time. Thank you.'

'That's really great to hear. And if you're enjoying it with this headwind, imagine what's it's going to be like when we turn back?'

We cycled another two miles beyond the beach until our watches ticked over the twenty-mile mark, before making a U-turn to begin the return journey to Roscoff. The difference was immediately noticeable, and for the first mile of the return journey I didn't even have to turn the pedals.

'This is amazing!' shouted Rachel.

Within no time we were back at the beach where we had stopped for wine, so stopped again, downed the remains of the bottle, and continued on our way.

It was surprisingly complicated to retrace our steps. Not only did we have to recognise each turning that we had made in reverse, but in order to make up the full 40-mile distance, we also had to retrace all our wrong turns and dead ends too. We were back in Roscoff just before 2pm and found an open crêperie where we devoured a savoury galette and a sweet crêpe each.

After lunch, we cycled out along Roscoff's pier or estacade where you can catch a boat to the car-free Île de Batz. About halfway out along the pier, the side wind became so severe that we had to dismount our bikes, fearing it was going to blow us over the railings and into the sea. It was a relief to return to the mainland.

With an afternoon at the spa to look forward to, I went to buy a bottle of wine in Roscoff to take back to our hotel. Every single shop in Roscoff had closed for the afternoon.

I knew there were some wine supermarkets on the outskirts of town, so offered to cycle out to one and meet Rachel back at the hotel.

'I'll come too,' said Rachel.

'Really?'

'Yes. You know me. I love cycling in France.'

'Ha, well you had disguised it very well until today.'

'I think I was just scared. I'm nervous cycling on the roads in England, and because I've not done any long bike rides in France, I didn't know what to expect. But cycling feels so much nicer and easier here for some reason.'

The French have a reputation for being a slightly curt and grumpy nation. But their respect for cyclists is phenomenal. In Britain, there is still a strong anti-cyclist contingent amongst the population, but the French attitude to cycling and cyclists is just leagues ahead of the UK. Not only do they make paths and marked routes the length and breadth of the country, but French drivers seem to be – almost without exception – cautious and respectful towards cyclists. Not once during our two days' cycling in France (nor my three days with Simon) did a vehicle pass too close to us, cut us up, or overtake at an inappropriate place. French drivers seem to universally accept cycling as a worthy form of transport.

The key seems to be to get more people cycling. This is not only important because more people cycling means fewer cars on the road. But the more cyclists we have on the roads, the more accustomed drivers get to sharing the road with bikes. Also, because I think experiencing the road from a cyclist's point of view can help make you a more empathetic driver.

I hope that I've always been sensible and courteous with cyclists while driving, but it wasn't until I started cycling on the roads regularly that I could empathise with how scary it can be on a bicycle. Being brushed by a bus on a tight bend, hitting a pothole, or being tailgated too closely up a steep hill all makes you feel incredibly vulnerable as a cyclist. Perhaps all drivers taking their driving test should be required to do a quick cycling 'experience' in order to get a better understanding.

I realise I am painting car users as the villains here and cyclists as some sort of unprotected heroes. Don't get me wrong, there are plenty of cyclists out there who are grade-A arseholes who don't do themselves – or their fellow cyclists – any favours in improving their reputation. Taking up too much of the road, jumping red lights, holding up traffic unnecessarily and excessively, being poorly visible, undertaking – many of which I have probably been guilty of at some point in my life – just add fuel to the fire and create a level of vitriol that will be hard to shake.

It's a two-way problem. Drivers undoubtedly need to be more aware and show more care on the roads with regard to cyclists, but cyclists need to respect car drivers too and do everything they can to help salvage something from the relationship.

Where are the jokes, George? What's with the long and boring rant? Why have you gone all Chris Boardman on us? Sorry, that was just a minor public service broadcast while it was on my mind. I'll try not to let it happen again.

The wine supermarket was, as the name suggests, a supermarket-sized shop that only sold wine. Thousands and thousands of bottles were stacked up in boxes and display cases all around the warehouse.

'What shall we get?' asked Rachel.

'We might not have much choice,' I whispered.

'What do you mean? There are literally thousands of bottles here.'

I looked around to make sure the shop assistants were out of earshot.

'We need one with a screw-cap. We don't have a corkscrew.'

Rachel laughed.

'Ok, that makes things a bit easier.'

We started browsing the aisles, ignoring all names, grape types and price tags, and looking only for screw caps. In the UK, screw caps now dominate the wine shelves, but the French still stubbornly refuse to accept the screw cap as a viable alternative to the cork. We weren't fussy and didn't need a selection. We only needed one bottle.

'Bonjour. Ça va? Can I help you?' said a shop assistant in perfect English. I imagine almost all of his customers are Brits.

I looked at Rachel. I couldn't bring myself to ask him

where the screw cap wines were.

'Bonjour. Ça va bien merci. We are just looking. Merci.'

He smiled, nodded and walked back over to the till.

We spent several more minutes scanning the aisles with no success. Then Rachel called in a loud whisper from the other side of the shop, 'George, I've found one.'

I walked around to meet her and found her pointing at a bottle of Lambrini.

I snorted. Lambrini – the cheap pear cider, sold in bottles that make it pretend to look like sparkling wine – was Rachel's drink of choice for most of her university life. Lambrini is produced in Liverpool, so I've no idea how it made its way onto the shelves of a French wine shop. Maybe it is considered classy in France?

'We're desperate, but not that desperate,' I said.

Eventually, after a few more minutes searching, I found a bottle of Chilean Cabernet Sauvignon, tucked away on a tiny '*New World*' shelf at the very back of the shop. It was three euros.

I ashamedly took the bottle up to pay and averted my eyes from the look of contempt on the face of the cashier as he scanned my wine. We had spent 15 minutes in a French wine shop, filled to the brim with lovely looking wines from across France, and we were leaving with a three-euro Chilean screw cap.

To make matters worse, while at the till I noticed they sold corkscrews for just two euros. But by that point it was too late, and the damage had already been done.

Did Not Enter

The Brittany & Spa Hotel is a striking 17th century former sea merchants' property which was rebuilt stone by stone in the 1970s. Our lovely room looked out onto the harbour and beach below. For the first time in my life, I got to wear a hotel dressing gown and slippers and walk down through the building to the spa area. We were the only two there and spent half an hour in the small swimming pool, jacuzzi and sauna, before reclining on the loungers and drinking some weird cucumber water. Our ferry back to Plymouth departed at 10pm the following day, so this was to be our only night in the hotel.

'We can have a late check out tomorrow if you like and just stay here all day,' I said.

'Don't you want to do some more cycling?'

'I don't mind. What do you want to do?'

'This spa is nice, but I think half an hour is plenty. I'm already a bit bored, to be honest. I would much rather go cycling.'

'Am I imagining things, or are you now choosing to cycle in Storm Gareth rather than a spa day?'

'It's possible I was overly pessimistic about this trip.'

Later that evening, after a couple of glasses of our Chilean red, we strolled back into the centre of Roscoff where I had booked a table at a tiny little restaurant called Le Brise Lames that had been recommended to me. The three set courses of the *Menu du Jour* was one of the best meals we had ever eaten. We also ordered a lovely bottle of French wine. It had a cork and everything.

'Happy nearly birthday,' I said, toasting my glass to Rachel.

'Thank you. Turning 40 doesn't seem so bad after all.'

'40 miles in Storm Gareth today was very good going. How far do you want to cycle tomorrow?'

'I guess we should try to do another 40,' she said.

'Cheers to that!'

It was pouring with rain when we woke the following morning, but we stretched out our visit to the extensive breakfast buffet for as long as we could, sampling almost everything on offer, and by the time we finished eating, the rain had stopped.

'Where are we cycling today?' said Rachel.

'Are you absolutely sure you don't want to go to the spa?'

'I'm absolutely sure I don't want to go to the spa. Although, I'm not sure how I'm going to cycle anywhere after that breakfast.'

We checked out of the hotel and retrieved our bikes from the hotel's laundry room where we had stored them overnight.

'I was thinking of heading along the coast the opposite way to where we went yesterday,' I said.

'Sounds good. Is that what you did with Simon?'

'The first bit of it might be, but a lot of the route Simon and I followed went inland. Let's just follow the coast as closely as possible like we did yesterday. But towards Morlaix instead.'

The wind had conveniently changed direction overnight. It was still blowing at about 40mph but was now coming mostly from the east. So, like yesterday, we would cycle into a headwind for the first half of the day, but we would hopefully have a tailwind for the return journey.

From Roscoff we followed little back roads and tracks along the coastline to Saint-Pol-de-Léon, before cycling quiet rural roads with crops growing either side of us. We were vaguely following signs along a small section of the Tour de Manche – a 435-mile loop around Northern France and Southern England – which, like my trip with Simon on the Eurovelo 4, threw up the occasional fun surprise. One minute we would be on a beautifully tarmacked road, the next we would be wheeling our bikes through thick mud, probably exacerbated by the recent rain. After one particularly exhausting section of mud that was impossible to cycle through, we reached a long beach close to the town of Carantec and I remembered I was carrying a third of a bottle of the Chilean screw-cap wine. As was now traditional for our late morning break, we sat on the beach and swigged it from the bottle.

We followed the Tour de Manche signposts around the narrow back streets of Carantec before a fantastic long stretch of road alongside the Morlaix river estuary. We had covered 20 miles long before reaching Morlaix, but Rachel was happy to continue on to the town centre at the lure of a good lunch.

We arrived in Morlaix at 2pm just as all the cafes and restaurants were closing, but we found a little burger shop imaginatively called Burger Shop. It was a fast-food restaurant manned by a lone man. This resulted in it being the slowest fast-food restaurant in the entire world. It was worth the wait, though, and we were rewarded with an incredible burger with all the trimmings, crispy fries and a bottle of cold French lager.

We then bought a selection of cakes and pastries from a nearby patisserie, ate half, and squashed the others into our rucksacks to eat on the way back. Check-in for our ferry was from 9pm, but there was also an option of an earlier check-in window between the hours of 6-7pm.

Despite our bulging waistlines and light heads from the wine and beer, the way home was relatively easy now that we were wind-assisted. Our kids had given us a shopping list of things they NEEDED us to buy from a French supermarket, such as sugary cordials, Pez sweets and giant Babybel cheeses. This additional stop meant it was going to be extremely tight whether we made it to Roscoff in time for the early check-in.

It was Saturday afternoon and the E'leclerc supermarché in Saint-Pol-de-Léon, where we usually stocked up on French food and wine before our ferry home, was closed, so we detoured into the town centre to a Super U and did a mad trolley dash to get everything we needed. I couldn't resist buying a couple of bottles of wine, a selection of cheeses and some chocolate, naively forgetting we still had to cycle to Roscoff.

The weight of my rucksack was so heavy that I was now almost fully reclined on my bike. Thankfully, the weight of the wine, hanging in a bag from my handlebars, helped keep my front wheel on the ground. The wind had picked up, but it was thankfully still behind us as we had 15 minutes until they closed the early check-in. It didn't matter too much if we missed it, but it would mean sitting in the ferry port car park for two hours, rather than in the bar on the ferry. We knew which we would prefer.

We covered those remaining three miles in less than ten minutes, screeching into the ferry port just in time. We had surpassed our 40 the previous day with 44 very windy miles.

On board the quiet ferry, we enjoyed steak frites and a bottle of wine (with a cork) in the restaurant and were tucked up in our cabin bed before most of the other passengers had even boarded the boat.

Although I had not admitted it, in the weeks before we came to France, I too had been slightly reluctant to go. For all the same reasons as Rachel, but also because Leo's new football team had a match scheduled for the Sunday morning. My mum and dad were going to take him, but this was only his second ever game and I was gutted that I might miss it. However, being on bikes, we were first off the ferry in Plymouth at 8.30am the next morning, first through passport control, and we made it to Leo's match just in time for kick-off.

'Thank you so much for an amazing weekend,' said Rachel.

'You're welcome. Did you enjoy it?'

'I loved every bit of it. Sorry for being so grumpy about it. It was very unfair of me.'

'I'm sorry for not booking a marathon in Europe instead.'

'That was honestly so much better than a marathon. It's made me quite excited about turning 40 now.'

'Aw, that's good to hear.'

'What do you want to do for your 40th?'

'I don't really need to think about it yet,' I said smugly. 'I'll still be in my 30s for a couple more months.'

Did Not Enter

EIGHT

A couple of weeks after returning from France, we took part in the Taunton Marathon, which was Simon's second attempt at sub-4 hours. Simon asked me to help pace again, and this time Rachel ran with us for added support. It was a much hillier route than we expected, and despite a promising start, the wheels fell off from about 17 miles and it was a slow and emotional finish. We finished in 4h 09m, which despite being an impressive four-minute PB for Simon, was nine minutes slower than he needed to fulfil his ambition. The hunt would go on, and I knew Simon would achieve his ambition at some point soon.

We all continued to enjoy our life back on the farm in Devon. Having assumed we would be there for a year or two, we had now been in the same house for almost six. Our landlords' son and daughter-in-law moved back from Spain with an assortment of cats and dogs to help with the running of the farm, and there was always lots going on.

Our cat Moomin started following us on our daily dog walks. She would see us all walking up the drive with Ludo and the three dogs from next door and think '*cool, that looks fun. I'll come too*', and then trot along behind for the two-mile loop. The two border collies are obsessed with Moomin and stalk her closely the whole way. Moomin doesn't seem to mind — perhaps enjoying the attention — and gives them a quick swipe with her claws if they get too close.

She often gets spooked by a cow or tractor, however, and disappears into a neighbouring field to hide. We've continued on, expecting her to follow, only to reach home without her. Then it's got to 11pm at night and I'll have to redo the walk in the dark, calling for her along the way. She will eventually emerge from a bush looking relieved that I finally came back for her, and we'll walk back home together.

The usual loop we do is all off-road so very safe. Things get a little more problematic when Moomin tries to follow us on family bike rides. You might think it would be impossible for a cat to keep up with bikes, but with an uphill in whichever direction we turn, at least one of the family is usually pushing their bike within the first few minutes, giving Moomin plenty of time to catch up. She then trots after us until we've either disappeared too far ahead, or until a car comes and she dives into the hedge. She will then wait where we left her until someone comes back for her either at the end of the ride, or late at night when we've realised she hasn't returned home. These instances don't seem to faze her, and she'll happily then join us for the next walk or bike ride, too.

During the Easter Holidays, we headed to North Cornwall for a few days' holiday in a static caravan.

'Have you done your yoga today?' asked Rachel, as we all sat around playing cards after dinner on the first night.

'Oh, damn, no,' I said.

I quickly discovered that yoga and caravans are not the greatest of friends. It was dark outside and pouring with rain, so I had no choice but to do it in the caravan. There was barely any room in any of the bedrooms to stand up, let alone perform any sort of yoga pose, so the lounge area was my only option.

It didn't go too well. Leo and Kitty decided that now would be the perfect time for them to have a pillow fight around me, Ludo was busy humping my leg throughout, and each time I stretched out an arm or a leg I either knocked over a glass, punched or kicked a child or dog, or almost put my foot through the television. Until this point, I had associated my daily yoga challenge with moments of peace and serenity. In an instant, this was flipped on its head. Yoga was now a type of endurance challenge. And it was a challenge that I wasn't sure I was up to. That first session in the caravan was 38 minutes, and it was the longest 38 minutes of my life. The next day's session was going to be 50 minutes. With the forecast looking wet all day, I didn't think I could face another session of caravan yoga, so I decided to take a temporary yoga break while on holiday.

'You failed,' said Layla, when she heard me tell Rachel my decision.

'What do you mean? Failed at what?'

'Your yoga challenge! Doing yoga every day!'

'Well, not really. My challenge was to do yoga every day in January. That's 31 days. I've done 98.'

'Yes, but then you did another month and another month. And now you've stopped.'

'Yeah, whatever,' I sneered.

I didn't want to admit it, but Layla was right. I had failed. Initially, it had been a month-long challenge, but it had developed into something more long-term. But it's not like I intended to do yoga every day for the rest of my life. The streak was going to be broken eventually, and I actually felt an enormous sense of relief to be free from the commitment for a while. At the time, I felt no disappointment or sense of failure at taking a break from my yoga challenge, and genuinely believed it was only a short hiatus. I would pick up where I left off as soon as we got home.

But I didn't.

Without that daily challenge and the incentive of the unbroken streak, my desire to resume yoga and pick up where I left off had diminished completely. I'm embarrassed to say that I didn't do a single session of yoga for the next eight and a half months.

Did Not Enter

The poor weather didn't last too long, and despite me being a yoga loser, we had a brilliant week exploring the local area and enjoying our first time away with Ludo, which added a whole new level of fun to the holiday.

I took him out for a walk/run one morning, along footpaths and quiet country lanes, down to the seaside village of Rock, which sits on the opposite side of the Camel Estuary to Padstow. All of Ludo's encounters with other dogs until now had been very positive. He was very sociable and loved meeting other dogs. But there were some seriously angry dogs in Rock. It's like they all knew Ludo and I were tourists and 'not from these 'ere parts'. We passed a particularly terrifying little terrier with massive rage issues. It flailed around on the end of its lead with the owner desperately clinging onto it like she was flying an out-of-control kite. Ludo and I gave it a wide berth and about 20 metres further down the road we passed a man and his large doberman cowering in an alleyway just off the road.

'Morning,' I said.

'Has she gone yet?'

'Who?'

'That lady and her dog. We pass her every day and I swear her dog is going to kill mine one of these days.'

I looked up the road and the lady and her miniature velociraptor had crossed to the other side of the road.

'Yes, the coast is clear. You're safe.'

'Thank you,' he said, looking genuinely terrified.

Following the foreshore for a while, we attempted to take a slightly different route back to our holiday park but found ourselves completely lost. It seemed that perhaps some of the locals were not too keen with us grockles walking the local footpaths so had removed the signs from their posts. On a couple of occasions, I entered fields over stiles and did a couple of full circumnavigations before concluding there was definitely no exit from the field – at least, not one that was marked. Instead, Ludo and I had to climb gates, squeeze through hedges, and shortcut across people's driveways, which is also presumably not appreciated by locals.

We had covered over seven miles by the time we got back to the caravan which was much more than Ludo should have been doing at his age. I had been telling Rachel for weeks not to overdo it with Ludo's exercising, and now I was the one overdoing it. But he had had the best time, and it was me that was flagging for the final couple of miles rather than him. It had been a joy having Ludo as a running partner. He was, in many ways, the perfect running companion: always available for a run, even with no notice; relentlessly positive and enthusiastic; keen to explore new routes and trails; fully appreciative of being outside and not too talkative. Although, at least with a human running partner, you don't have to pick up their poos.

When I said 'not too talkative' you might think Ludo would or should not be talkative at all. I confess that Ludo was given his own voice by all the family soon after we got him. All the family except Layla, who refuses to acknowledge that Ludo can talk. It takes Layla a huge amount of self-discipline to not converse with Ludo when he asks her a question in his ridiculous gravelly voice. The rest of the family will happily have long conversations with Ludo, but Layla steadfastly refuses to stoop to our level. In all the time we have owned him, she has slipped up just once. While out on a walk with Layla holding his lead, I asked her, sorry, I mean Ludo asked, 'Layla, can you let me off my lead now please?' and she replied 'No, Ludo.' She realised and regretted her lapse immediately, but it was a momentous occasion and Ludo was delighted that Layla could hear him after all.

.

NINE

The prospect of turning forty had fazed me very little. It is only a number, and although I predictably feel the years slipping by quicker and quicker, I also feel fitter than I have done in many years and extremely grateful to be healthy. And I will always be younger than Rachel.

'What are you going to do for your 40th?' people kept asking me.

'Oh, nothing. I'm not into celebrating my birthday,' I would reply.

'But you have to do SOMETHING. It's your 40th.'

'It's just a normal birthday.'

They were right, though. I had to do SOMETHING. And if I didn't arrange something, then something would be arranged for me. And I really hated that idea. Even a couple of low-key drinks in the pub would suddenly become an occasion, or a quiet meal at home with the family would become my 40th celebrations, and although that would suit me perfectly, I felt it might be an anti-climax for Rachel and the children. I thought I needed to find a way to at least attempt to mark the occasion.

Did Not Enter

The obvious solution and distraction from having an actual birthday celebration was some sort of sporting activity. If I was out and about doing something physical for the day, then I wouldn't be able to have any other type of celebration. Basically, I was in denial and looking for a way to escape turning 40.

What could mark the occasion better than running 40 miles for my fortieth? I did some googling and stumbled upon the Ridgeway 40: an event organised by the Long Distance Walkers Association (LDWA) along the ancient Ridgeway between Wiltshire and Buckinghamshire. 40 miles is quite an unusual length for a run, and not only was the distance perfect, but it was taking place on my actual birthday. It was fate. 40 miles would be the furthest either Rachel or I had ever run, and it seemed like a fitting way to celebrate the occasion.

The Long Distance Walkers Association, as the name implies, was established for people wanting to walk long distances. But as the popularity of ultra-running increased, the LDWA was happy to allow runners to take part in their events. Because of the fast pace of many walkers, and slow speed of some runners, the boundary between runners and walkers is often blurred.

Founded in 1972, the LDWA now has almost 10,000 members across 43 regional groups around the UK. As well as providing routes and group walks, the LDWA also arranges many 'challenge events' each year – such as the Ridgeway 40 – which are organised walks that include marshals and often refreshments.

The Ridgeway is claimed to be Britain's oldest road. Largely following the chalk ridge of the Berkshire Downs, it has been a popular route for traders, farmers, travellers and armies for over 5,000 years.

Midway through our only other ultramarathon together, I thought our marriage might not even survive until the end of the race, and the chance of us running any others together was zero. But by the end of the run, we both thoroughly enjoyed it, and when I suggested the idea of the Ridgeway 40 to Rachel, she seemed oddly delighted by the idea.

I didn't want to spend my birthday weekend away from Layla, Leo and Kitty, and as Wiltshire is too far to travel from Devon and back in a day, we decided to make a weekend of it. Rachel's parents agreed to join us for a couple of days and look after the children while we ran. I booked us all a couple of rooms in a hotel that just so happened to be called The George Hotel and was in no way an egotistical attempt for me to milk the hell out of my birthday.

The event started in Avebury in Wiltshire and followed the crest of the Ridgeway east towards Reading, ending in the village of Goring on the banks of the River Thames. Our hotel was about four miles from the finish, so Rachel and I planned to drive to Goring early on the Saturday morning, catch the provided bus to the start, do the run, and then have the van waiting for us all at the finish. Rachel's parents and the children would spend the afternoon walking the four miles along the Thames from our hotel to meet us at the finish.

Our phone alarms sounded at 5.00am on the other side of the hotel room. Rachel only half-stirred, so I got up and turned off both. Layla, Leo, and Kitty had spent the night in their grandparents' room next door, so they could escape the early wake-up call.

'Happy birthday!' said Rachel, mid-yawn.

'Thank you.'

'Got anything nice planned today?'

'I thought we could go for a little run.'

'I'm so excited,' she said, with genuine enthusiasm. My enthusiasm for endurance events takes a while to get going. It is always elusive at 5.00am. Even on my birthday.

'Do you want the first shower?' I asked.

'No, you go ahead, birthday boy.'

The water was only lukewarm, so I was in and out within a couple of minutes. I dried myself off and reached into my bag to retrieve my running clothes and felt a strange rustling sensation. I pulled out my t-shirt to reveal four giant birthday badges (because one badge would not be enough) pinned to the front, complete with rosettes and lots of frilly ribbons.

'Oh god,' I sighed. 'What have you done?'

'Happy birthday!' said Rachel.

'Do I have to run in these?'

'Of course you do. It's your birthday. There's something else in there for you, too.'

I reached my hand back inside the bag and pulled out a big fluffy hat in the shape of a birthday cake with furry candles sticking out the top.

'Happy birthday!'

'Oh joy. This day keeps getting better and better. Any other surprises?' I said, as she unzipped a big holdall and pulled out a helium balloon with a big 40 on it.

'Oh, hooray. Do I have to run with that too?'

'Well, not if you don't want to, Mr Grumpy. But I think you should. It is your birthday, after all.'

'You don't even like people singing *Happy Birthday* to you on your birthday, and you want me to turn up at an organised event covered in badges, wearing a novelty hat and carrying a helium balloon?'

'Basically, yes.'

I sighed and gave half a smile.

'Can I at least put the balloon and hat in a bag until we get to the start? The idea of a bus full of strangers singing *Happy Birthday* to me at 6.30am is too much.'

'Ok, fair enough. How come turning 40 has made you so grouchy? Do you promise you'll wear it all for the run?'

'Fine,' I conceded. 'I promise.'

We parked on a side street in Goring and walked across the Thames (there was a bridge) to the neighbouring village of Streatley where we joined a queue of other walkers and runners waiting for the bus.

The LDWA attracts an incredibly eclectic mix of people. Despite turning 40, Rachel and I were definitely on the younger end of the spectrum. There was a wide spread of ages, each person choosing to spend their Saturday walking or running 40 miles. In the days leading up to the Ridgeway 40, lots of friends and family wished us well and thought it was an impressive and fitting birthday challenge for us, but not one of them implied it was something they would like to do. It was reassuring to suddenly be surrounded by hundreds of people who had also decided that this was a good way to spend their day. And, unlike me, these people were not just trying to escape their 40th birthday celebrations. With my lightweight jacket zipped up to my neck to hide my badges, my hat in my rucksack, and my helium balloon in a carrier bag, we slipped onto the bus, drawing no-one's attention.

The bus ride took over an hour, driving on fairly big roads at a decent speed. It was daunting and strangely surreal to think that we were soon going to be running the same distance (though thankfully not on roads) back to where we caught the bus.

The bus parked up outside the village hall on the outskirts of Avebury, and the driver wished us all luck with a mixture of respect and bewilderment. We collected our race numbers and timing fobs, which we would need to scan at the start and finish, as well as five checkpoints along the way. Entrants could start anytime between 7.45am and

8.45am. They encouraged faster runners to wait until closer to 8.45am to ensure that the checkpoints were all open. We knew there was no risk of us arriving at the checkpoints too early, as we were unlikely to be much faster than the walkers.

There was no danger of us starting too early anyway, as Rachel joined a queue for the ladies' toilets that stretched almost 40 miles. I went to the loo three times while she waited.

I pulled on my giant cake hat, removed the balloon from the carrier bag and secured it with the long ribbon to the top of my rucksack. We had our timing fobs scanned by a marshal – who didn't seem to notice or care about my birthday attire – and we were off.

'Round to the left,' said another marshal, pointing us down the side of the village hall.

We proceeded around to the sports field behind the village hall and could see a group of about six women all walking across the grass towards a gate on the other side.

'Love the hat! Is it your birthday?' one said, as we jogged past them.

'Yes,' I said proudly. '40 today!'

'Happy birthday!' they shouted.

We reached a small lane and assumed there would be a marshal or arrow directing us which way to turn. There was neither. We could see no other runners or walkers in either direction.

'Which way do we go now?' asked Rachel.

Did Not Enter

'No idea', I said, as I began to amble up the lane to the right, hoping to see a marker or some clue.

By this point, the group of women had also reached the lane and started walking in the same direction as Rachel and me.

'Is this the right way?' one of them said to the others.

'It must be,' said another. 'Birthday boy looks like he knows what he's doing. Let's follow him.'

'No! Don't follow me!' I shouted. 'I've got absolutely no idea where we are going.'

'Well, we are all going to follow you.'

'NO! I can't handle this responsibility.'

I pulled out a copy of the route map I had printed off from the race website to use in case we got lost. I didn't expect this to happen within the first 100 metres. The map was a hand-drawn squiggle of a 40-mile route, condensed down to fit on one piece of A4. It was impossible to establish from looking at it which way we were required to go. Rachel and I carried on walking up the lane as it felt wrong to come to a complete standstill. Another walker caught us.

'Is this the right way?' he said to the group of women.

'We hope so. We are just following Balloon Boy.'

I was no longer birthday boy. Now I was Balloon Boy.

'Balloon boy has no idea where he is going,' said Balloon Boy, talking about himself in the third person. 'Don't follow him!'

At this point, another runner passed us. He was holding

a map and looking purposeful.

'Let's follow him,' I said.

'No, don't follow me!' he said. 'I don't know where I'm going.'

'Well, you look like you do, so we are following you.'

Rachel and I jogged behind him, and the walkers followed in our direction.

'Stop following me!' he joked. 'I honestly don't know where I'm going.'

'Neither do we. We'll follow you.'

As we had already discovered, LDWA events are fairly low-key when it comes to signs and route markings. Most long-distance walkers are well prepared and have decent maps and a basic understanding of navigation. We, clearly, did not.

'Someone mentioned something about crossing a main road,' said the runner.

'That looks like a main road,' I said, pointing to what looked like a main road.

'Great, let's cross it.'

In the distance we could now make out another person with a backpack, which suggested we were going the right way. Either that or we were following a random walker, or another clueless navigator.

A couple of minutes later we found our first sign for the Ridgeway on a gatepost and realised for the first time we were heading in the right direction.

'See, I knew we should follow you,' I said to the runner.

'That was a complete fluke. I'm Ben, by the way.'

'Hi Ben. I'm George, and this is Rachel.'

'Hi. I was going to ask if you've done this before, but I think I already know the answer.'

'This will be the furthest we've ever run. What about you? Have you done many ultras before?'

'I've done a 50-mile walk, but this will be my furthest run.'

The balloon had been flapping around my head since the start, but as we picked up our pace slightly, it seemed to become less of a nuisance. I turned to look back just as the thin silky ribbon slipped free from my bag and the balloon floated up into the air.

'NOOOO!' I shouted. 'MY BALLOON!' I ran after it, jumping as high as I could, trying desperately to reach it and missing by a mere 10 feet.

'OH NO! Balloon Boy's lost his balloon!' I heard the group of women shout further back down the track.

'What happened?' said Rachel. 'Did you do that deliberately?'

'Of course I didn't. I tied it in a double knot. All of that tugging and jerking as we ran must have caused the ribbon to undo itself.'

When Rachel had given me the balloon, I confess that the thought of running 40 miles with it had not been too appealing. But after I tied it to my bag, I embraced the birthday celebration and was enjoying the added challenge of running with a helium balloon. I also quite liked being known as Balloon Boy. Now, as I watched it drift up over the Wiltshire countryside, I felt like a catastrophic failure. I had carried the balloon for less than a mile.

I was also consciously aware that I was littering the countryside. Only a week earlier, I had picked a 'birthday boy' helium balloon out of the sea while swimming and tutted at the disgraceful and irresponsible 'birthday boy' who had let go of his balloon and allowed it to drift out to sea. Now I was the disgraceful and irresponsible birthday boy. There was nothing I could do about it now, and I had to try not to let it ruin the day.

Ben, the other runner, had been running along with us chatting about his two children with a third on the way. We were all getting on really well and it felt like he would make a fun additional running companion for the day. He told us of his upcoming Scafell Pike marathon and a few other events he had planned. But as soon as my balloon floated up into the sky, it was like his opinion of me changed. I had disappointed him. He quickened his pace, sped up the hill, and we never saw him again.

The path joined the main Ridgeway after a mile and a half, and the route became more clearly defined. We climbed gradually as we overtook a steady stream of walkers who had set off earlier and presumably not wasted time getting lost at the start. The track was wide and rutted, but there was plenty of room to run on the grass and dried mud on the verge. Below us, fields of wheat and rapeseed stretched out in every direction.

Did Not Enter

Most walkers we passed wished me a happy birthday after seeing my hat, and I was now making the most of the occasion. These walkers didn't know about my balloon and that I was a massive loser.

The weather was perfect. There was very little wind, and a thin layer of cloud was holding off the early morning sun. Within the first couple of miles, Rachel stopped and removed some of the multiple layers she had put on, during which time many of the walkers overtook us again, only for us to go through the Happy Birthday charade when we passed them again.

At Barbury Castle, we passed through the ramparts of the old iron age fort, and from there we were required to follow a diversion on footpaths and bridleways for a few miles before rejoining the Ridgeway at Whitefield Hill.

There was a vague description of the diversion on our map, and we climbed a series of stiles and networked through a few different footpaths and bridleways. We had not seen another person since leaving the Ridgeway at Barbury Castle, so had to trust our instincts that we were going the right way. Thankfully, on this occasion, our instincts were correct, and we eventually met the main road and found Checkpoint 1, having covered a distance of 10 miles.

'Happy birthday,' said the first marshal to meet us. He was a man I also recognised from being at the start in Avebury who seemed to have some role in organising it all.

'Thank you. I'm 40 today. 40 miles seemed like a good

way to celebrate.'

'You don't look a day over 50,' he said, very proud of his own put-down.

'Ha, thanks.'

'You're welcome.'

The checkpoint was also a well-stocked refreshment stop with jugs of squash, plates of biscuits and bags of crisps. Doing their best to be as environmental as possible, the LDWA ask all runners to bring a mug with them. Rather than use single-use plastic cups at each feed station, runners and walkers simply fill their own cups from the jugs. I delved into my backpack to retrieve mine, which I had stupidly buried under five rounds of sandwiches.

'We've decanted big sacks of crisps into small paper bags to minimise the waste and do our bit for the environment,' said another marshal.

'That's fantastic,' I said, trying not to think about my stupid helium balloon, which was probably already suffocating a rabbit somewhere in neighbouring Hampshire.

We walked up the long hill from the checkpoint while eating our crisps and got chatting to a walker we had caught up with.

'What time did you set off?' I asked.

'I'm not sure. Just before 8am, I think.'

'Well done. I can't believe it's taken us 10 miles to catch you. Have you walked since the start? You must be the first walker.'

'Yes, I don't do running. I'm trying to average just above 4mph for the whole thing. It's going ok so far.'

It was an impressive pace to maintain, and I struggled to keep up with him even for that short uphill section. Towards the top of the hill, I looked back and realised Rachel had dropped quite far behind.

'Good luck,' I said to the walker as I stopped to wait for Rachel. 'Hopefully we will catch you up again in a bit.'

Rachel is a great runner. But she is a terrible walker. I don't mean that she's bad at walking. She's just very, very slow. If I am running up a hill and decide to walk, I'll try to maintain a bit of pace and the change of stride is often enough to get my breathing under control. Rachel goes from racehorse to shire horse in a split second.

'Are you ok?' I said, as she eventually caught me up. 'Sorry, I was chatting to that guy and I didn't realise you weren't with us anymore.'

'I'm good, thanks. Just plodding along.'

'Having fun?'

'I'm having a brilliant time. Are you enjoying your birthday?'

'I'm really loving my birthday. Thank you!'

The top of the hill signified the end of the diversion as we re-joined the Ridgeway and soon overtook the walker again. Most of the Ridgeway is closed to vehicles as it is completely unsuitable terrain, but soon after re-joining it we had to pause to let three Land Rovers pass, only for them to decide that it was unsuitable for them too and we stood and watched as they each did an awkward twenty three-point-turn in the hedge.

A little further along, a small man appeared from a footpath to our left.

'Got lost,' he said, sounding very flustered. 'So, so lost.'

'Oh no, what happened?' I asked.

'Went wrong way. A long, long way that way,' he said with a foreign accent, possibly South American.

'Well, you're going the right way now. It's only the Ridgeway between here and the finish. Apparently it should be easy to follow.'

He trotted off into the distance. Despite having a backpack, he was carrying a bag of sandwiches in one hand and his water bottle in the other, as though he had been interrupted mid-picnic.

The heat had really picked up. The morning cloud had long since dispersed and the sun blazed down on us. It is very exposed on the Ridgeway and there is little tree cover to provide any shade.

'You must be sweltering in that stupid cake hat,' said Rachel.

We had been running for two and a half hours and I had forgotten I was even wearing it.

'Now you mention it, my head does feel a bit weird.'

'You don't have to wear it the whole time, you know,' she said.

'But I'll feel like a failure if I take it off.'

'Why?'

'Because you wanted me to wear it.'

'I didn't expect you to run the whole way in it. I didn't think you would run at all in it. It was only a sort of joke.'

'Why am I wearing it then?'

'I don't know.'

'So you won't think I'm a failure if I take it off?'

'No of course not,' she said. 'You've already failed by losing your balloon.'

'Oh, please don't remind me about my balloon. I never thought I could feel so attached to a balloon.'

'If you were properly attached to it, it would not have floated away.'

'Very funny. I definitely can't take my hat off now, though.'

A few miles further down the track, the odd South American man emerged from a bush, still gripping his bag of sandwiches and looking very confused.

'Got lost,' he said.

'Again?' we said.

He looked at me strangely, not realising we were the same people who had been on the trail when he last got lost. He didn't reply and hurried off into the distance with his sandwiches.

About five miles later he overtook us yet again, looking even more agitated.

'Where did you come from? Did you get lost again?'

He muttered something to himself in Spanish and trotted off ahead. Having taken a wrong turn in the

EnduranceLife South Devon ultra the year before, Rachel and I had some sympathy for how easy it is to get lost. But that was only once. And we had not been following a fairly straight, well-defined path.

'How the hell does he keep getting lost?' I said to Rachel.

'I don't know. It's one path the whole way. All you have to do is follow it. It is very funny, though.'

'And we thought we were bad at navigating.'

We reached another checkpoint at about 20 miles and the race marshal who had earlier told me I looked 50 was there again.

'He's 40 today,' he told the other marshals. 'He's going to look 60 by the end of today.'

They all burst out laughing and I chuckled along too, just to humour him, but fuming inside that the same marshal had roasted me twice in one day. The idiot.

The terrain of the Ridgeway varied considerably and seemed to change every half mile, alternating between gravel track, grass, rutted mud, and chalk. It kept things interesting as the trail undulated through the countryside. At some point, we unknowingly crossed into Oxfordshire.

At the halfway point, we passed over the top of the famous Uffington White Horse. There are many white horses carved into hillsides around the UK (the majority can be found in Wiltshire), but the Uffington White Horse is widely considered the oldest. It is believed to have been carved into the chalk hillside almost 3,000 years ago.

Despite passing only metres from the monument, we couldn't actually see it as we were just over the crest of the hill above.

From the 20-mile point onwards, having been running mostly on our own for several miles – apart from the South American sandwich bag man – we started to notice a lot more walkers and runners. Many of them were kitted out with rucksacks and walking poles, but we assumed they must just be ramblers visiting this popular stretch of Ridgeway. It was then that we noticed most of them had the same timing chip as ours tied to their bags, meaning they were taking part in the same event as us. *But how could these people have walked for 25 miles with big rucksacks and still be ahead of us when Rachel and I had run most of the way?*

'They must have just started really early, I suppose,' said Rachel.

'Or maybe we are just REALLY slow,' I said.

It was very demoralising as we thought we had passed the last of the walkers ages ago and that it would only be runners ahead of us for the rest of the day. Yet now we were suddenly alongside lots more walkers.

We continued to be bewildered by these walkers' incredible stamina until almost the 30-mile point, when I really started to question things. We approached a group with the same timing chips, all ambling along at a very slow pace, chatting and laughing together as though they were just on a jaunt to the pub. *Surely they MUST have set off the night before?*

'Excuse me,' I said, as we ran alongside them. 'What time did you all set off?'

'10.30,' one of them said.

'10.30pm last night?'

'No,' they laughed. '10.30am this morning.'

'This morning? That's two hours after us. Did you start at Avebury?'

'No, no!' they laughed. 'We started at White Horse Hill. We are doing the Ridgeway 20.'

'The Ridgeway 20? Oh, thank god for that. I didn't even know the Ridgeway 20 existed. We've been passing all these groups of walkers and wondering how they were all so far ahead of us.'

'Ha, I take it you're doing the 40?'

'Yes.'

'Well done.'

'Thanks. Well done to you. Enjoy the rest of your day.'

Rachel and I both laughed and felt a big sense of relief that we weren't as slow and crap as we thought.

The feed stations were so well stocked that we need not have brought our own food with us. I had seriously over-catered and made five rounds of sandwiches, nearly all of which lay untouched in the bottom of my rucksack.

Rachel's rucksack was tiny and useless. I was carrying all of our sandwiches and two big bottles of water, which we both shared and topped up at the checkpoints. I assumed Rachel was just carrying a few of her own snacks in her bag, but after about 32 miles, she admitted she had been carrying two small bottles of prosecco in her rucksack the entire way.

'Why didn't you tell me?' I said. 'We could have drunk them earlier.'

'We could have them now, if you like?'

'Are they not a bit warm by now? And you've basically been shaking them up for the last six hours.'

'Yeah. Sorry about that.'

'Thank you, though. That's very sweet of you. What else have you got in your bag?'

'A bag of crisps and thirteen bars.'

'THIRTEEN BARS? What the hell? How many of them have you eaten?'

'Er... none.'

'So, have you actually used ANYTHING that is in your bag?'

'Erm... no.'

'So you could have run this without carrying a rucksack at all?'

'Er... yeah, I guess so.'

'So you've basically been using me as your packhorse?'

'You're my husband.'

'Packhorse.'

'Whatever.'

Despite walking painfully slowly up hills, Rachel more than makes up for it on the flats and downhills, and we seemed to be fairly evenly matched for running long distances. We both had our low moments but were able to take it in turns to motivate each other.

For large sections of the run, we could see sprawling towns and villages below us, reminding us we were passing through the middle of a heavily populated area of England. But high on the Ridgeway, we passed no more than half a dozen houses between the start at Avebury and the outskirts of Streatley where the race ended.

'We can still break 8 hours,' I said, looking at my watch.

'I thought you weren't bothered about how long it took us?'

'I'm not. But it would be quite nice to do it under 8 hours, wouldn't it?'

'Yeah, I guess that would be good.'

Part of me loved the fact that there were no expectations or time constraints. Some would take a full 14 hours to walk the route. 40 miles is 40 miles, however long you take. So it felt good not having the added pressure of a time goal. But part of me also thought it would be nice to achieve the 8-hour time we had loosely estimated at the start. Without a target, there was little incentive to keep running up each and every slight incline. There was little incentive to run at all.

'I don't really mind how long it takes us,' I said.

'As long as it's under 8 hours?' said Rachel.

'No. Well, I mean, under 8 hours would be a bonus.'

'Fine, let's pick up the pace. It is your birthday.'

My other motivation for finishing faster was that I was looking forward to seeing Layla, Leo and Kitty (and the in-laws, of course) and us all going out for dinner. The quicker we got to the finish, the more time we had to celebrate.

The mid-afternoon heat had become a little too much for me in my cake hat, so I removed it for a couple of miles, but at the final checkpoint – about four miles before the finish – I pulled it back on.

The last couple of miles were gradually downhill as we came down off the Ridgeway towards the banks of the River Thames. Our legs were feeling ridiculously tired and weak, but we knew we were nearing the finish line, so tried to summon a last bit of enthusiasm. For miles 38 and 39, we clocked 9-minute-miles, which we felt incredibly proud of as they were our fastest of the day. My watch read 7h 57m as we reached the outskirts of the village of Streatley, and it felt like we would comfortably get in under eight hours. My watch then ticked over to show we had completed 40 miles, but there was still no sign of the finish.

We caught another runner and he seemed surprised by our energy as we passed him. Checking the results later, it transpired that he had started his race 15 minutes after us so could have crawled to the finish line and still broken 8 hours.

'Where is the finish line?' said Rachel as we reached a junction. I spotted an arrow pointing left and we followed it down the high street.

'It must be here somewhere,' I said, as I looked

desperately at my watch. It said 7h 59m 30 seconds. 'We've got 29 seconds!'

'WHAT?'

'29 seconds before 8 hours.'

'NO WAY!' shouted Rachel. 'WHERE IS THE BLOODY FINISH?'

'I thought you didn't mind how long it took us?'

'WELL, I DO MIND NOW!'

She broke off into a full-on sprint, but there was still no sign of the finish. By now, I knew it was a lost cause. The volunteers at each checkpoint along the route had spent several precious seconds trying to scan our dirty timing fobs, so even if we found the finish, our time would be over eight hours by the time we officially finished.

'Excuse me, do you know where the finish is?' Rachel said hastily to a pedestrian.

'Down in the village hall over the bridge.'

'Thank you,' she said, dashing off.

Goring and Streatley are two villages joined by a bridge over the River Thames. We had come down off the Ridgeway into Streatley, but the finish line was actually in Goring. As we crossed the bridge, I made the rash decision to stop my GPS watch on 7:59:59. Yes, technically, I was cheating. But I didn't care. It was my birthday, and I could do what I liked. We had run a total of 40.5 miles and still not reached the finish line. We had completed our 40 miles well inside our own self-imposed 8-hour mark, sticking to our planned average speed of 12 min/mile. I didn't care that I was a fraud. Just don't tell Layla.

As we approached the village hall we saw Layla, Leo, Kitty and Rachel's parents standing at the edge of the road. They were all cheering and holding a big *HAPPY BIRTHDAY* banner. As we reached them, they each fired a party popper at us.

'WELL DONE!' they shouted. 'HAPPY BIRTHDAY!'

'Thank you!' I said. 'Aw, it's so lovely to see you all.'

'Where do we get our timing-chip scanned?' said Rachel rather abruptly, who, for someone that didn't care at all about her finish time, seemed to care an awful lot about her finish time.

'Inside the village hall,' said her dad. 'Quick, go and get it scanned.'

It took a predictably long time to get out fobs scanned, and I was glad I hadn't been relying on those last precious seconds otherwise I might have strangled one of the elderly volunteers. As it was, our official finish time was 8h 03m.

I felt a tap on my shoulder.

'Happy birthday,' said a voice, and I turned to see a runner who I recognised as the man we ran past on the way to the finish.

'Thank you. Well done.'

'This is a gift from your running partner,' he said, handing me a £20 note.

'What? My running partner?' I said, not sure what he was talking about.

'The lady you were running with. This fell out of her

pocket after you sprinted past me.'

'Oh wow, thank you. That's really honest of you.'

'You're welcome.'

'Rachel! This fell out of your pocket when you were running. That guy saw it and picked it up.'

'Oops! Wow, that was good of him. Do you know what? I felt that £20 in my back pocket earlier and thought it would be lucky to still be there at the finish.'

'And you didn't think that at that point maybe you should put it somewhere more secure?'

'Like where?'

'In your rucksack?'

'No, there are no small pockets in my rucksack.'

'It doesn't matter. You didn't even open your rucksack for the entire 40 miles. It would have been perfectly safe in there.'

'That's true.'

Rachel's mum and dad had brought a bottle of prosecco (this one was cold and unshaken), and Rachel's mum had baked a delicious chocolate cake. They sang *Happy Birthday* and we sat and ate cake and drank prosecco for half an hour in the village hall.

As we were leaving, 40 minutes after finishing our race, the South American guy who we had last seen disappearing into the distance ahead of us staggered into the room looking completely bewildered. He was shaking his head and still clutching his bag of sandwiches.

'I got lost. AGAIN,' he said. 'I hate the bloody

Ridgeway.'

He overtook us about three times during the run. We never once overtook him. Yet we somehow finished 40 minutes ahead of him. I think he must have run at least 50 miles, although I've no idea where. I doubt he knows either.

Rachel drove us back to the George Hotel and we found a nearby pub where we all ate some great pizza, drank good beer and wine, and I opened lots of lovely presents. We were sharing a room with the children for the second night, so I bought a bottle of wine from the nearby shop, and we returned to our room to watch *Britain's Got Talent* to end a memorable day.

I had spent my 40th birthday running 40 off-road miles with my wife through three counties of the beautiful British countryside. Turning 40 felt pretty damn good.

Sharing a room with Mummy and Daddy was too exciting for Kitty, and she secured a spot in the double bed with Rachel, so I got relegated to the single. Leo lay in the bed to my left, snoring heavily throughout the night. Kitty lay in the bed next to me to my right, flailing around in her sleep every few minutes. At one point she smacked her open water bottle off the bedside table, soaking me in my bed, with the rest of the bottle emptying out onto my clothes, which I had left in a pile on the floor.

At 5.00am, just as I was finally drifting off to sleep, Rachel's bloody phone alarm – which she had not switched off from the day before – blared out from the other side of the room. She was in such a deep sleep that I had to get up to switch it off. An hour later, as I finally began to fall asleep again, the children were all awake and ready to start the day.

Turning 40 was a bit shit after all.

TEN

Rachel, Layla, Leo and Kitty all found a new activity that kept them amused for a lot of the summer: dog shows.

Ludo was quite limited to the categories he was eligible for. Prettiest, most obedient, cutest, most handsome would never be the categories for him. He was more of a 'novelty act' dog, entering categories such as 'scruffiest' and 'fancy dress.' At one local show, we dressed Ludo and a friend's dog as a bride and groom, and they had a spectacular play fight in the judging ring. It was not the best start to their married life, but quite amusing for the audience.

What I assumed was going to be a one-time thing, seemed to have become an almost weekly occurrence during the school holidays. Our days were shaped around where there was a dog show. Rachel would suggest a walk out in some obscure village we had never been to before, and it would later transpire that there happened to be a village fete on which included a dog show. *What were the chances?* And there was a fancy dress round and Rachel just so happened to have an outfit for Ludo in her bag. *What luck!* We started to recognise all the familiar faces on the dog show 'circuit'. You know, the weirdos who think their dog is more special than everyone else's and choose to spend their weekends desperately seeking approval from the judges.

And then I realised that was us.

We were those weirdos who thought our dog was more special than everyone else's. And we were choosing to spend our weekends desperately seeking approval from the judges. It was a good excuse to get out and about in the sunshine, though, and the children all loved it. And our dog clearly was more special than everyone else's.

We taught Ludo a couple of simple tricks, like rolling over and offering a high-five. At another dog show, Layla took Ludo into the ring, confident that her roll and high-five routine would impress the judges. The elderly lady next to Layla got her Yorkshire terrier to roll over about eight times consecutively. Ludo had only ever managed one roll at a time. Layla looked at us helplessly when it was her turn.

'Just try to get him to keep rolling!' called Rachel from the ringside.

Layla got him to roll over once and then he gave his high-five before reluctantly doing another half roll and another high-five. It was somehow enough to scrape third place.

'The next category is Dog Most Like Owner,' said the announcer at one fair we attended.

'This should be funny,' I said.

Did Not Enter

'It will be,' said Leo.

The compere read out a list of dogs and owners, including what sounded a bit like 'Ludo and George'.

The kids and Rachel all sniggered.

'What did she say?' I asked.

'She said Ludo and George,' said Layla. 'You better go and join the others in the ring.'

'Are you serious? Did you enter me?'

'No, Ludo entered himself!' said Rachel. 'Of course we entered you!'

'You are all SO annoying. Do I really have to go up there?'

'YES!' they all shouted.

Ludo and I made our way around the ring and joined the others in the middle. There were about twelve of us humans, and going by the proud smiles on everyone's faces, it was clear they had all chosen to enter themselves, rather than being signed up against their will.

I assumed this was a novelty joke category and the judges would take a quick glance around the ring and then hand out a token rosette. But each of the three judges were taking it extremely seriously and moved around all the competitors at an excruciatingly slow pace. They paused next to Ludo and me, scrutinising us both thoroughly without a hint of irony.

We miraculously walked away with a third-place rosette. I didn't know whether to be pleased or insulted. They awarded second place to a lady whose hair was the most unnatural shade of brown I have ever seen. She had clearly been to the hairdresser and got them to do a colour match of her spaniel's ears. They awarded first place to a young ginger-haired boy and his ridiculously cute red cockapoo puppy called Teddy.

I think the rest of the family could feel my enthusiasm for dog shows waning. They began discussing categories and tactics without including me in conversation, and the four of them would sneak off together to do last-minute rehearsals without me. Then at one show we attended, they unveiled an entirely new routine that I hadn't been privy to. It involved all three children curled up in a ball on the floor, interspersed a couple of metres apart. Rachel then ran with Ludo by her side, and he was supposed to jump over each of the children in turn. He jumped over Layla, bypassed Leo in the middle, and then jumped over Kitty. I was actually quite impressed. Especially as they had somehow colluded in secret to practice the trick without me knowing. Unfortunately, I was more impressed than the judges, and despite a good response from the crowd, Ludo didn't even make the top three. From that point on, the rest of the family's enthusiasm for dog shows thankfully diminished too.

ELEVEN

During the summer, Layla set herself the challenge of swimming outside every single day of the school holidays. She went to the beach with some friends on the first day while I took Leo to a football tournament, and it was on the second day that she announced her intentions for the challenge. As Layla was the only one of the family to have swum on the first day, she could tell us proudly we had already failed – failed to complete a challenge we didn't even know we were taking part in. But we all liked the sound of her challenge and were keen to join Layla for the rest of the summer and see how far we could go.

It proved to be possibly the most enjoyable summer holiday break we had ever had, thanks largely to Layla's swimming challenge. Whatever the weather, we would have to incorporate a swim into the day somehow.

One evening, almost a month into the challenge, we were all watching TV at about 8pm, when Layla remembered we hadn't been for a swim.

'We might have to leave it today,' said Rachel.

'But then I will have failed my challenge.'

Rachel and I had both had a couple of beers so we couldn't drive anywhere, so it would either mean a long evening walk or bike ride to a beach. Or, more likely, the end of Layla's challenge. A severe weather warning had also been issued and people were advised to stay away from the coast.

'I'm really sorry,' I said. 'I don't know how we forgot today.'

'But I've not missed a day in 27 days.'

'I know. It is very frustrating for you.'

'There must be somewhere I can have a swim.'

'What about that small pond up in the field by the road?' I said, only half joking.

'That one where the dogs sometimes jump in to cool down?' asked Rachel.

'Yes. It's not very deep, but that would count as swimming, wouldn't it?'

'Can we go there? Please?' begged Layla. 'Can we? Can we?'

'Yeah, I suppose so,' I said. 'I'm sure Mummy's up for a dip.'

'Ha, no thanks. I've already failed, remember? I missed day 8, as well as day 1, so you guys are on your own.'

So, Layla, Leo and I walked through the wet and windy farmyard in our swimming costumes, much to the amusement and surprise of our neighbours. Rachel and Kitty walked up to watch and laugh at us.

The pond, when we reached it, was smaller than I

Did Not Enter

remembered. It was about 6ft long and a couple of feet wide, which made it just big enough for a human.

'What counts as swimming?' I asked.

'I guess we just have to lie down in it,' said Layla.

'The shoulders have to be submerged,' said Rachel confidently. 'It doesn't count unless you are lying all the way down with your shoulders in the water.'

'Alright, when did you suddenly become the authority on wild swimming?'

'About a minute ago when I saw how disgusting this pond looks.'

The word pond makes it sounds nicer than it is. It's where a stream comes under the road and then flows into a small muddy pool where cows gather to drink. The surrounding area was all squelchy and cow-trodden, and the cows had left their marks and their 'marks' all around.

'Who is going first?' said Layla. 'I think Daddy should.'

'Oh, do you now?'

I pretended to feel hard done by but was secretly relieved to go first. Partly to get it over and done with, but also because I could see how muddy the water would get once the ground was disturbed, so was keen to take advantage while it was slightly less revolting.

I dipped my toes into the already soupy water, and it felt noticeably colder than the sea and estuary. One stride took me out into the deep end, which still came up below my knee.

'Right, here goes,' I said, sitting down in the water and

leaning back. 'Does this count? Am I in?' I gasped.

'No, further. Your shoulders are still sticking out,' said Rachel.

'How about now?' I gasped.

'That's good, but you have to hold it for a few seconds.'

'What? Why?'

'Otherwise, it's just a splash.'

'Right, done,' I said, sitting up.

'Daddy didn't do any swimming,' said Kitty.

'What do you mean? I just lay down in a pond.'

'But you didn't actually do any swimming strokes. You have to go swimming every day. Sitting in a pond doesn't count.'

'Mummy said I just had to get my shoulders wet.'

'Kitty is right,' said Rachel. 'Layla's challenge is to swim every day, not just get wet every day. I think you need to make a few swimming strokes.'

'Really?'

'Yes,' said Kitty. 'Otherwise, you have failed.'

Layla and Leo stood there shivering, remaining silent, knowing they were going to have to do whatever I did.

'Fine. I hate you,' I said, wading back into the pond and this time lying down on my stomach, and making a few token breaststroke movements with my arms.

'Happy now?' I said.

'I suppose that counts,' said Kitty.

Leo went in next and stood for several minutes with the water up to his knees, arms hugging his upper body tightly

Did Not Enter

to try to keep warm.

'It's actually not too bad,' I lied. 'I might go back in and do a few more lengths.'

'Ok. Count me down,' said Leo.

'Three... two...'

'No, count me down from five.'

'Five... four...'

'Actually, start at ten.'

'Oh, hurry up! I'm getting bored now,' said Rachel.

'Fine,' he said, dropping from a standing position to flat on his stomach like he was doing a burpee. He made a few 'strokes' kicking up even more of the stinking mud from the bottom.

'Brilliant, well done,' said Rachel as Leo climbed out.

'Your turn, Layla,' I said

Layla just stood there, staring at the pond.

'I'm not sure I want to. It smells disgusting.'

'We only came up here for you. You better go in now.'

'Yeah, Layla. You'll have failed your swim challenge,' said Leo.

'Well, you already failed! You missed day one. I've done 27 consecutive days now.'

'So have me and Daddy now. And if you don't swim today and we swim tomorrow, we will have done 28.'

Layla gave Leo a confused look, as though he was talking rubbish.

'He's right,' I said. 'We missed day one, but as of now, we have swum the same number of days as you. The only way you can stay ahead of us is to get in that pond!'

This was enough motivation to get Layla in. Going by the consternation and determination on her face, I expected her to throw herself into the water without a moment's hesitation, but instead she stood there faffing around for ages. Leo and I were getting very cold. She eventually lay down, did a few strokes, and we hurried home for hot chocolates, wrapped in our towels and much to the confusion of our now even more surprised neighbours.

As the local beaches filled up with holidaymakers on the hottest days, we headed out for several walks on Dartmoor instead, each time incorporating a river or lake into our route.

There's a popular spot on the River Dart where families gather for picnics and barbecues, and swim and jump from the rocks into the river. We had planned to head up there one weekend, and Layla had made arrangements for a friend of hers to join us. On the day, a storm closed in with lightning, thunder and heavy rain forecast for the rest of the day. But with Layla's commitment to her swim challenge, it meant that the weather would not stop us. So we headed up to Dartmoor, the rain pelting down the entire way.

'Why are we doing this?' asked Leo, looking out of his window.

'It'll be fun!' I said, unconvincingly.

'The weather is awful!' said Kitty.

'There's no such thing as bad weather...' I said.

'WE KNOW!... there's only inappropriate clothing,' said Leo. 'You always say that. It's such a stupid phrase. This is obviously VERY bad weather.'

Rachel and I looked at each other and acknowledged he was right. The weather was horrendous and even if we had decent waterproof clothing (which we didn't) it still wouldn't be appropriate.

'Well, I think a swimming costume would be appropriate,' I said. 'It's designed to get wet.'

We pulled into the car park and sat there for a few minutes while the rain battered the windscreen. We had driven all this way, so we might as well go for it. And Ludo was desperate for a walk, so at least one of us was going to have to venture out.

'The weather forecast said it is going to brighten up in about half an hour,' I said, trying to remain optimistic.

We set off through the woods and 10 minutes later, as we approached the swim spot, the rain stopped, the clouds parted, and the sun appeared for about half an hour. We had the river all to ourselves and had a magnificent swim.

'You picked a good day for it,' said a lady walking by with her dog.

'Yes, we got lucky with a break in the weather.'

'I walked through here yesterday and there must have been over 200 people here.'

We felt very fortunate to be the only ones there. And it

was all because we had a commitment to swim because of Layla's challenge.

Another day, we went for a walk during torrential rain for a swim on a different stretch of the River Dart. This time, the rain didn't stop and in fact got heavier once we all climbed into the river. It made the walk and swim even more memorable, though, and if it hadn't been for Layla's challenge, swimming would have been the last thing on our minds.

The last week of the school holidays was spent in Portugal to celebrate my dad's 70th birthday with my parents and my sister's family. With the Atlantic Ocean – warmed by currents from the Mediterranean – only metres from the hotel, Layla's swim challenge didn't prove too problematic for the week.

It was our first ever all-inclusive holiday, and we took full advantage of all the food and drink. My highlight of the entire holiday also happened to be Rachel's worst moment.

We were at the pool bar mid-afternoon and there was an assortment of buffet items laid out for a snack, just to tide us through the hunger-gap between the two-hour lunch and the multiple course dinner.

'Do you want me to get you a plate of food?' I asked Rachel, as I got up to go to the buffet.

'No thanks. I'll just share yours.'

I rolled my eyes.

Did Not Enter

I returned with a selection of cold meats, cheeses and olives and we sat and chatted with my parents, sister and brother-in-law. I picked up a cocktail stick that was skewered through a piece of melon and a cube of what looked like serrano ham. I put it into my mouth and the soft melon melted away in seconds. The meat was more challenging. I chewed it for several minutes but didn't seem to be making any progress, so I subtly removed it from my mouth, and as discreetly as possible, rested it on the edge of my plate.

We carried on talking and drinking until our plates were empty. Well, all except my piece of chewed up meat.

'Don't eat that piece,' whispered Rachel. 'It's really chewy.'

I let out an uncontrollable boom of laughter and found it genuinely hard to breathe.

'What's so funny?' she asked.

'That meat!' I said. 'I know it's chewy. I've already chewed it!'

'What do you mean?' she said, before the realisation hit her. 'Wait. You mean...'

'Yes. It was SO chewy. I chewed it for ages, but I gave up and tried to hide it on the edge of the plate.'

'Oh my god! I feel a bit sick now. So, I've been chewing a piece of meat that you had already chewed?'

'Yes!'

The rest of the family now understood what had happened and were all in hysterics. All except Rachel, who looked in a state of complete shock.

'Oh god, that is so gross. Why would you do that?'

'Do what?'

'Chew it and then put it back on the plate.'

'That's what you did!'

'Yes, but at least I warned you about it.'

'I thought it would be obvious it was chewed. It didn't exactly look appetising.'

'I honestly think I might throw up.'

'Well, maybe next time you should have your own plate.'

TWELVE

Having taken a break from the same old familiar events – the Dartmoor Classic, Cotswold 113 triathlon, Exeter Marathon – there was no resisting signing up for my fifth visit to the Cornish Marathon in November. The lure of the hoodie and pasty was too strong.

The year had started so well for my fitness. I began by running 10k every single day in January. I had a 98-day streak of doing yoga every day. Rachel and I cycled 84 miles in France and then ran 40 miles for my 40th birthday in May.

And then I did very little for the rest of the year.

Just when I was feeling fitter than ever, I let it slip. Most of the time that I had previously spent running or cycling was now taken up with twice daily dog walks. Not that I was complaining. The routine of walking Ludo became one of my favourite parts of the day. I enjoyed my walks so much that many of my runs also turned into walks. In fact, walking was often the best thing about running. I loved seeing Ludo's enthusiasm at the mention of a walk, or just the sight of me putting my shoes and socks on. It was definitely contagious, and although I had run very little in the second half of the year, I had probably spent more time outside than ever.

But dog walking was not really conducive to marathon training. Rachel and I did both go running with Ludo occasionally. He enjoys running, but the runs are very stop-starty with lots of sniffing, urinating and pooing. And Ludo is almost as bad.

We had been invited to dinner the night before the Cornish Marathon to celebrate a friend's birthday.

'Shame we can't make it,' said Rachel.

'Why can't we make it? My mum and dad are already looking after the children because of the marathon the next day.'

'Er... yeah... we can't go because of the MARATHON the NEXT DAY.'

'So? That doesn't mean we can't go, does it? We don't have to stay late.'

'Well, I'm not going to go. I already told Cath earlier that we couldn't make it.'

'Oh, I've just sent Ben a message telling them I can.'

I went along without Rachel, planning to only stay a short while, and I definitely wouldn't drink, and would be home in bed at a decent time. I of course ended up staying very late, having way too much to drink, and not getting home until the early hours. But I had a brilliant night and as I staggered home, I was confident I had made the correct decision and that baked camembert, beef bourguignon, red wine and several dark and stormies was actually ideal pre-marathon preparation. I was going to smash it!

When my alarm sounded early the following morning, I knew I had made a big mistake.

'I'll drive,' said Rachel disapprovingly as I met her in the kitchen.

'Are you annoyed with me?'

'No, why would I be?' she said in a way that meant 'yes'.

'I don't know. Because I went out last night?'

'No. It doesn't matter to me. Did you have fun?'

'I did, thanks.'

'How are you feeling?'

I didn't answer.

In the days leading up to the race, there had been substantial rainfall and the River Fowey subsequently burst its banks. A large part of the marathon route runs alongside this river and the day before the race, the road was still impassable. There was a suggestion the race was going to be cancelled, but the organisers managed a significant last-minute route change so that it could go ahead. The course was now an out-and-back along the first half of the original route. This half was significantly hillier than the second half, meaning the new route would be notably tougher. Even in its previous incarnation, the Cornish Marathon had declared itself '*the UK's toughest road marathon*'. But I couldn't complain. In previous years I had found the four-mile section that ran along the River Fowey one of the hardest parts of the day. There was something demoralising about a long straight road, especially when you've covered 16 miles already. Also, because you are following the river, it has the appearance of being flat, but as the road follows the river upstream, it is heading very slightly uphill the entire time.

I dozed in the car while Rachel drove, and we made it to the start in Pensilva in plenty of time. There was no sign of marathon legend Danny Kay, whom I had chatted to at each of my previous Cornish Marathons. Perhaps he too was hungover somewhere after a night on the lash.

As soon as we started running, I felt considerably better. It was a cool misty day, and the fresh air and breeze on my face was making me feel a little more human. Rachel and I had not discussed it, but I knew she would be running her own race and would not be slowing down for me and my self-inflicted malaise.

We ran together – mostly in silence – and I was able to hang on for the first nine miles. Then in an instant I knew that my time was up. I would not be able to keep up with Rachel any longer.

'You go ahead,' I said. 'Good luck!'

On previous occasions when I had got to this stage, Rachel would say something like, *'are you sure?'* or *'shall we run together?'* or at least something vaguely sympathetic. This time she simply said 'ok' and stepped up a gear, without even looking back.

It was a proper kick in the teeth, and I was furious with myself. Not just because I hadn't been sensible the night before, but for letting my fitness slip and allowing Rachel to move so far ahead of me. Because I secretly knew that even if I had gone to bed sober the night before at a reasonable time, I would most likely have still ended up in this situation, possibly just a couple of miles further up the road.

This anger and frustration continued for a few minutes, but I soon got over it. I don't think I had ever run an out and back race like this, and it was a double-edged sword. In the first half, you get to see all the people ahead of you in the race, and it feels quite demoralising. I was heading down a long steep hill, and the race leaders were coming up the other way at a significantly faster pace than I was running down. To rub salt in the wounds, one guy in the top 20 was running wearing flip-flops. These runners were all several miles ahead of me. The first few all looked like elite athletes: tall, lean, and long-legged and had physical attributes that I wasn't born with (particularly the women). But a lot of them looked no different to me. Just fairly average looking men and women who had put in the hours to train. It was inspiring to see what can be achieved with some dedication and determination.

I passed Rachel coming back the other way after she had passed the turnaround point. She was already a fair distance ahead of me and gave a brief wave and a smile.

My mood dipped again. But after passing the turnaround point, I got an instant lift as now everyone I passed was behind me. It had a dramatic effect on my mindset. So what if Rachel was ahead of me? She deserved to be. She had put in the effort to train and was currently much fitter than me. And although my fitness had certainly slipped, I was still running a marathon. Not only was I running a marathon, but I was running a marathon with an almighty hangover.

What a legend!
I am the man!

Despite the circumstances, I was actually really enjoying myself. The weather turned against us in the second half, with the wind and rain coming from every direction, but it acted as a literal and metaphorical slap in the face and was strangely invigorating.

On one of the many long uphill sections, I dropped to a slow walk and pulled out my phone. There were several messages in the group chat from the previous night's birthday meal. All my friends were comparing how they were feeling.

'Hangover from hell!'
'I'm too old for this shit.'
'Worst headache everrrrr.'
'Regretting that last dark and stormy. Forecast for the day: dark and pukey.'

I sent them a selfie of me looking rain-soaked and

bedraggled mid-marathon, which instantly made them all feel happier with their own situations.

I wrote: *'Rachel left me at 9 miles. 17 miles done. I'm eating soggy hula hoops and walking.'*

'That is so sad,' replied one.

'I hope you enjoyed your evening enough to make your current situation worthwhile,' replied another.

I certainly did. I had no regrets. Well, perhaps that final dark and stormy. Meeting up with friends the night before was more important than getting a slightly quicker time for the marathon. If anything, it was actually beneficial as it gave me something to blame, rather than my lack of training.

Rachel completed the marathon in 3h 59m, which was a fantastic time for a course with 2,600ft of climbing. Despite my fitness slipping behind Rachel, it was pleasing knowing that I could show up at a marathon feeling worse for wear and still get around the course. I got a second wind towards the end (must have been that last dark and stormy) and crossed the line in 4h 10m, which was technically a Cornish Marathon PB for me. However, the last-minute route change seemed to have resulted in a course that measured at least half-a-mile short of the full marathon distance. We'll gloss over that minor detail.

Having taken part in about 20 marathons, it was also refreshing to have reached the stage where I could turn up on the morning of the race without the sense of nervousness or intimidation that I used to feel. With far fewer organised events on the calendar over the last 12 months than previous years, this year's Cornish Marathon felt more special than usual. Even with the hangover. In fact, the hangover inadvertently made me feel like I had achieved an important mental transition in how I approached physical challenges. It's often a difficult balancing act to combine a social life with training or competing, and although drinking too much and getting too little sleep the night before a big event won't become a pre-race tradition, it was nice to have been able to do both, without one hugely impacting the other.

I enjoyed taking a break from most of the tried and trusted events I had entered over the previous years and had not missed the races I did not enter. There were plenty of other adventures that took their place instead. Two cycling trips to France. A fleeting love affair with yoga that ended badly (but I hoped would one day be rekindled). The Ridgeway 40, which proved that running a long way can be a fun way to celebrate a birthday. Layla's swim challenge had given me a new appreciation for regular cold-water dips, and as the end of the year approached, Rachel and I were still swimming in the sea at least once a week. My 10k a day in January had already got me excited about repeating the challenge next year. And getting Ludo had made me realise how much I love walking.

Did Not Enter

Things were looking promising for 2020. I had so many exciting plans: ultra-marathons, my first ever swim-run event, a big family cycling adventure, holidays abroad, lots of books to write; new adventures that would push me and test me like never before. Everything was wonderful in the world. 2020 was going to be such an incredible year. I could not wait.

What could possibly go wrong?

Author's note

Thank you for choosing to read my book. If you enjoyed it, I would be extremely grateful if you would consider posting a short review on Amazon and help spread the word about my books in any way you can.

You can get in touch via social media:
www.facebook.com/georgemahood
www.instagram.com/georgemahood
www.twitter.com/georgemahood

Or join my mailing list on my useless website to be the first to hear about new releases.
www.georgemahood.com
Signed copies of all of my books are available in my website's 'shop'.

Did Not Finish is a series of books. Please read on…

Did Not Enter

Book Six...

Did Not Happen – book six in the *DNF* series – is available to order on Amazon.

Here is the blurb…

As a new virus sweeps across the globe, George and Rachel are faced with their biggest challenge yet.

The year begins positively with George and Rachel running every single street of their local town. Just days before the country goes into lockdown, they take on the 20 miles of the Grizzly. A race so muddy that firefighters are stationed at the finish line to hose down runners.

Then the year takes a dramatic turn.

Food shortages, homeschooling, quiet roads, home haircuts, yoga, Rachel's new marathon a month challenge and a walking holiday… in a different part of Devon.

2020 is a year none of them will ever forget.

Did Not Finish is a series of books about George and his family's adventures in running, cycling and swimming. From ultramarathons to triathlons, 10k swims to European cycling adventures, George promises fun and laughter every step, pedal, and paddle of the way.

BOOK **SIX** IN THE **DNF** SERIES

DID NOT HAPPEN

ᴹᴵˢADVENTURES DURING A GLOBAL PANDEMIC

2m

GEORGE MAHOOD

Acknowledgments

First thanks go to all the organisers, marshals and volunteers for putting on these races. Many of them stand outside all day in horrendous conditions, often with no reward or incentive other than the satisfaction of being a part of the event. And perhaps the joy of watching us suffer.

Special thanks to our family and friends who regularly step in to help with childcare while Rachel and I are taking part in these events.

Rachel's editing job for these books was not as scrupulous as usual, which she claimed was because she enjoyed them so much. I think that is only because she features so prominently in them. She would often write 'LOL' in the margin, even though she had been sitting next to me while reading and hadn't made a murmur. Anyway, thank you for lolling (internally).

Becky Beer was as ruthless as ever with the red pen during her proofreading. That's a compliment. Thank you! Please check out her Bookaholic Bex blog (www.bookaholicbex.wordpress.com) and Facebook page.

Thanks to Robin Hommel and Miriam for additional proofreading and feedback.

Thanks to all our friends who have taken part in these challenges and adventures with us. It is always reassuring to not be the only ones with a ridiculously stupid concept of 'fun'.

Thanks to Rachel… AGAIN (she's even got a starring role in the acknowledgements) for reluctantly agreeing to take part in many of these events with me. We are not always perfect running, cycling, swimming partners, but I wouldn't want it any other way.

Thanks to Layla, Leo and Kitty for putting up with your annoying parents and for continuing to inspire and amuse us. Hopefully one day you will look back and be glad we dragged you out on all these walks.

Thanks to my mum and dad for dragging me out on all those walks when I was younger. I didn't appreciate it at the time, but I do now.

Lastly, thanks to you for reading this series. The idea that people enjoy reading about random things I get up to still feels very bizarre to me, but I'm always honoured and grateful.

Big love.

Also by George Mahood

Free Country: A Penniless Adventure the Length of Britain

Every Day Is a Holiday

Life's a Beach

Operation Ironman: One Man's Four Month Journey from Hospital Bed to Ironman Triathlon

Not Tonight, Josephine: A Road Trip Through Small-Town America

Travels with Rachel: In Search of South America

How Not to Get Married: A no-nonsense guide to weddings… from a photographer who has seen it ALL

(available in paperback, Kindle and audiobook)

Printed in Great Britain
by Amazon